ALI IN BRITAIN

ALI
IN BRITAIN

Michael Tanner

**FOREWORD BY
MUHAMMAD ALI**

MAINSTREAM
PUBLISHING
EDINBURGH AND LONDON

First published in 1995 by
MAINSTREAM PUBLISHING COMPANY (EDINBURGH) LTD
7 Albany Street
Edinburgh EH1 3UG

ISBN 1 85158 760 8

A catalogue record for this book is available from the British Library

Typeset in 11 on 13pt Palatino

Printed and bound in Great Britain by Butler and Tanner Ltd, Frome

This book is dedicated to the memory of my 'old man' who, though not taking kindly to Ali at first (like many of his generation), soon saw the light and became mesmerised along with the rest of us.

Also by Michael Tanner

My Friend Spanish Steps
The King George VI Steeplechase
Teleprompter & Co
Great Racing Partnerships
Pretty Polly – An Edwardian Heroine
The Champion Hurdle
Dessie: A Year in the Life of Desert Orchid
The Major: The Biography of Dick Hern
Great Jockeys of the Flat
Michael Roberts: A Champion's Story

CONTENTS

ACKNOWLEDGMENTS

Putting this book together, on and off over a period of three years, has been a labour of love. It is not a commissioned work. Accordingly, I must thank Bill Campbell and Mainstream for sharing my faith in the project and allowing it to see the light of day.

Although Muhammad Ali has been the subject of numerous books, these have – unfortunately for British fans – paid mere lip service to Ali's many and varied adventures in this country. This regrettable oversight begged correction.

All manner of people were invited to reminisce about Muhammad Ali. One or two surprisingly uncharitable souls declined. To the many who freely gave of their time I extend my sincere thanks: Henry Cooper, Brian London, Richard Dunn and Jimmy Tibbs; Reg Gutteridge, Peter Dimmock and Jarvis Astaire; Jean Childs, Margaret Danskin, Muriel Oates and Sylvia Hogarth; James Blackburn, Rodney Smith, Jenny Urwin and Alyson Hiller; Paddy Monaghan, Nick Reekie, Perry Aghajanoff and Johnny Walker. I owe a particular debt of gratitude to the last four gentlemen who were kind enough to lend me photographs and memorabilia from their personal collections.

Michael Tanner,
Sleaford,
March 1995

FOREWORD

There will always be a special place in my heart for the people of Great Britain. Over the years, you have treated me with enormous kindness. Many of you stood with me during the difficult days of my exile from boxing. And it was in Great Britain that I had the privilege to meet two great competitors, Henry Cooper and Brian London.

Ali in Britain brings back many fond memories for me. I hope it does the same for you.

Muhammad

Berrien Springs,
Michigan,
May 1995

PREFACE

The man at the heart of this book is no saint but any search for disapproval or censure in the pages that follow will prove fruitless. This book pays unashamed homage to the owner of one of the best-known faces on the planet and to the special relationship he forged with this country.

All of us who grew to adulthood in the 1960s owe an incalculable debt to Muhammad Ali. For sure, he thrilled us and he entertained us. But more than that he confronted authority. Through him we teenage rebels bucked the system; thumbed our noses at the older generation. He won our respect and admiration inside and outside the ring. Boxing laboured under a certain dullness until he burst onto the stage and has never been the same since he left it.

Father Time extracts his dues from every one of us, Muhammad Ali included. Even so, to each and every one of us Muhammad Ali will always remain the quick-witted, sharp-tongued, fleet-footed, slick-punching Adonis who stole our hearts and minds back in the 1960s; a figure to whom we can with justifiable affection address the words of Bob Dylan:

May your song always be sung
May you stay forever young.

ROUND ONE

HE CAME, HE SAW, HE TALKED

Most of us in this country got our first real close-up of him on Wednesday, 29 May 1963. The man whose first utterance, 'Gee-Gee', had, according to legend, stood for 'God-Given', was due to appear on television: *Sportsview* 8.45 p.m., BBC, straight after *Z Cars* and immediately before the News. Just for once Britain's adolescent male population would have to forsake *Rawhide*, the cult western series on ITV.

Anyone with a genuine, rather than passing, interest in this programme knew why he was in Britain. They knew he was the 1960 Olympic gold medalist at light-heavyweight and the winner of all 18 of his professional bouts as a heavyweight. They were aware he was a good-looking negro boy of 21 hailing from Louisville, Kentucky, who talked so much and so colourfully that he had earned himself the soubriquet of the 'Louisville Lip'. 'I have a machine-gun left jab, a bazooka right cross and a dynamite uppercut,' he was wont to inform would-be interviewers, who seldom got a word in edgeways: 'I am the Greatest.' Singing his own praises came just as easily in verse as prose.

> *This is the legend of Cassius Clay, the most beautiful fighter in the world today.*
> *He talks a great deal and brags indeedy of a muscular punch that is incredibly speedy.*
> *The fistic world was dull and weary, with a champion like Liston things had to be dreary.*
> *Then someone with colour, someone with dash, brought fight fans all running with cash.*
> *This brash young boxer is something to see and the heavyweight championship is his destiny.*

Inside the ring he moved with the same fluency, a youthful arrogance compelling in its novelty and effectiveness. In a division populated by leaden-footed plodders there was no heavyweight remotely like him. Correction. There was no sportsman remotely like him. This mahogany Adonis – Harry Belafonte with extra muscles, according to one newspaper – had the opportunity to become the James Dean or the Elvis of boxing: an icon for an energetic post-war generation fast discovering its identity and the power of that identity. The Cavalier of Clout! Even before *Sportsview*'s

11

All smiles at Isow's restaurant as Henry Cooper makes the acquaintance of the 'Louisville Lip'. Bud Flanaghan and Jack Solomons (left) are much amused (Mirror Syndication International)

opening credits rolled and the familiar signature tune had struck up, those of school age just knew what the main topic – indeed, the *sole* topic – of conversation would be in the schoolyards and common rooms tomorrow morning. Did you see him? What do you reckon? My old man thought he was a right loudmouth and can't wait for him to get a hiding. The generation gap had forced its way between the ropes; the Swinging Sixties had found a standard-bearer in the world of boxing. Cassius Marcellus Clay had arrived in Britain.

He was here to take on south-east London's very own fighting greengrocer, Henry Cooper, the British and Empire champion, on Jack Solomons's Wembley promotion of 18 June. 'Promoting is easy,' said the cigar-chomping Solomons. 'What's difficult is making money out of fights.' With Clay in his corner Solomons could afford to be optimistic. Clay could draw a crowd like no one else. He made a point of talking up his fights, in the manner of the old adage: 'He who has goods to sell/And whispers of them down a well/Will not make as many dollars/As he who climbs a tree and hollers.' He ridiculed his opponents and predicted – frequently in rhyme – when they would succumb to his multifarious talent. 'Cooper's a tramp, a bum and a cripple not worth training for. If he talks jive I'll take him in five,' he boldly announced; on another occasion the couplet was

12

*What quickly
became an all
too familiar
scene on the
London streets
(Popperfoto)*

suitably tailored for his hosts, viz: 'When they queried me about the Cooper bout/I answered with Shakespearian thrift/When they asked me which round I'd knock Henry out/I answered Henry the Fifth!' Lastly, alluding to America's latest astronaut: 'Henry Cooper will think he's "Gordon" Cooper when I put him in orbit.'

Throughout the land Cooper was deferred to as 'Our 'Enery', an endearment which spelled out how passionately the British public longed to see Clay get his comeuppance. In the aftermath of a severe winter the country found in Clay's outrageous antics something to laugh at, as the BBC's boxing correspondent Harry Carpenter later recalled. 'And when I say laugh I mean it because at the time Clay was regarded as not much more than a big joke. True, he'd been Olympic champion and won all 18 of his pro fights, finishing most of them in precisely the round he said he would. But the idea one day he would be world champion, another of his predictions, was too laughable for words. A man who spouted poems and jigged round the ring like a lightweight, dropping his hands, couldn't be taken seriously.'

The match had been announced in April – 'Cooper v Clay is a Natural' blared the front cover of *Boxing News* on the 19th – after Clay had extended his unbeaten record to 18 by outpointing Doug Jones. British interest in a possible clash with Cooper had been sufficient for the BBC to dispatch Carpenter to New York prior to the Jones fight (due a *Grandstand* screening on 23 March) with orders to interview the rising star. Carpenter snared his quarry with a little kidology. 'I rang him at his hotel and put a proposition to him. "You call yourself The Greatest. Why not come with me to the top of the Empire State Building. We can talk there and tell people that The Greatest has met The Highest!" Clay loved the idea.' Cassius duly won the fight but not that impressively or as he had predicted. 'Jones bursts Clay bubble', opined *Boxing News*. Carpenter himself wondered whether Clay might be too flashy for his own good, a sentiment shared by fellow scribe, and later his counterpart at ITV, Reg Gutteridge. 'I covered the Olympics for the *Evening News* and thought Clay was a bit crazy. I wondered if he had any courage; whether he'd opt out in a rough ride. Normally, the flashy ones are not so brave. But he had as tough a draw as you could get in the Olympics: he met some hard nuts. How can he beat them, I asked myself? But beat them he did. I misjudged him.'

Others dispatched across the Atlantic with orders to run the rule over this mould-breaking young boxer were Sydney Hulls (*Daily Express*) and Peter Wilson (*Daily Mirror*). They caught up with Clay in a Los Angeles hotel: 'I'm going to be the perfect heavyweight champion – like the young Joe Louis. I'm clean living, I haven't got a prison record. I think you've got to be an idol for young people. I've told Liston I'll take him in eight. Even if I could beat him in the seventh I'd keep him dazed and then get him in the eighth!' Concluded Wilson: 'A show off? A loudmouth? Clay has been called worse than that. But, in this country, dedicated to the proposition that "you either put up or shut up", he has consistently put up. And most of what he says about himself is true. If he succeeds in this pugilistic pilgrimage then in two years I think Liston might have a real fight on his hands.'

The whirlwind that was Cassius Marcellus Clay hit – in every sense of the verb – Britain for the first time on 27 May. Solomons's advice to 'commence training your ears' proved no idle warning. First to suffer was the customs officer who had the temerity to enquire whether the young visitor had anything to declare. Besides £275 of excess baggage Cassius saw fit to add: 'The Cooper-Clay fight's set for 18th June/For Cooper any date's too soon/London Bridge is falling down/So will Cooper in London Town.' With that, the boxer and his entourage, which comprised bodyguard Ronald King, sparring partners Jimmy Ellis and Don Warner, assistant trainer Chickie Ferrara (principal trainer Angelo Dundee was in New York with another of his fighters, Luis Rodriguez, who was about to challenge Emile Griffiths for the world welterweight title) and his brother Rudolph Valentino Clay, were swept off to a 'Welcome to Britain' lunch in Soho.

The venue was Jack Isow's restaurant in Brewer Street, not far from Solomons's office. A front door made of cellophane had been specially constructed so that Clay could make a 'smashing' entrance. Awaiting him inside the restaurant were the gentlemen of the press and, of course, his opponent who was accompanied by his manager, the exceedingly droll Cockney Jim Wicks, nicknamed 'The Bishop' on account of his shiny bald pate, pink cheeks and venerable demeanour. The protagonists were separated at the table by Solomons and the deputed master of ceremonies, comedian Bud Flanagan. Membership of The Crazy Gang more than qualified Flanagan for this dangerous assignment, which became increasingly precarious when he deliberately chose to introduce the American guest of honour as an afterthought. Up leapt Cassius: 'Ah don't need no introduction. Everyone knows Cassius Clay!' he boomed before launching into the anticipated mixture – well rehearsed – of prediction and sales pitch. 'Why did you allow this nice kid to fight me? I'll ruin him! It's too bad. You shouldn't have allowed him into the ring with me. It'll be his last fight. Five rounds! That's all! If I don't win in five I won't go back to the States for 90 days. If I lose I'll retire. No, I don't want to shake hands with Cooper. I don't want to meet him till I get in the ring with him. Don't take that five too strictly. I might reduce it! Don't get there late! I might finish it all off in one. I'm here to sell this fight. I won't stop running till every seat is sold and I want them to put in some standing room, too. If this fight ain't a sell-out I don't fight! Can't you get that Cooper to say something? Is he that scared? I don't seem to be able to make anyone mad in England. You all keep laughing!'

The only occasion during the function Cassius paused to draw breath was when he passed Cooper's twin brother Jim sitting at the next table. 'Man, I thought I had seen a ghost,' he informed Henry. The British champion was unmoved. 'I came to meet him but all I've done is hear him,' he said, adopting a rolled-up napkin as an ear-trumpet. Today he chuckles at the memory. 'He was at his brashest then. He annoyed the press more than me. I just looked and laughed at him. You couldn't let his actions get to you because that's what he wanted.'

Clay may have annoyed the press but how it loved the raw material he was providing. Fleet Street was not about to look a gift horse in the mouth, especially one with a mouth like Cassius Clay's. 'Oh, Blimey! How Cassius talked' was the headline of a centre-page spread in the *Daily Mirror* penned by Peter Wilson. Universally known and respected as 'The Man they can't gag', Wilson did not pull his literary punches. 'There has never been anything like it. He came, he saw, he talked. If Clay fights one half as fast as he talks either Cooper will go out in record time or the kayo king from Kent will fall down himself exhausted and breathless.' Wilson could not resist concluding with a poem of his own:

15

'Boxing poet Cassius Clay
Hit the City yesterday,
Posing, shouting, full of action,
'Selling Clay, the big attraction.'

Alongside Wilson's piece was another from Ed Vale, describing how he had given Clay a guided tour of London. Buckingham Palace? 'It looks swell. I think I'd like a place like that.' The Mall? 'Broadway's wider than this.' An illuminated Piccadilly? 'When do they turn the power on, man?' After a bout of shadow-boxing, which brings the traffic in the Circus to a grinding halt, Cassius elects to move on. 'I want to visit one of your coloured quarters. I am interested in the social scene,' he says with a hint of what's to come. Post Brixton, the evening predictably climaxes with a foray into a Soho club where a 'hostess' requests a dance. 'I'm sorry, honey, but I only dance in the ring.' Vale then chronicles the man-about-town's return to his hotel for 'the second steak and fourth sleep of the day'. Just in case readers refuse to believe this pugilistic superman ever sleeps the *Mirror* prints a large photograph of a slumbering Cassius. Even The Greatest has to recharge his batteries! And Monday, 27 May, had been some day for, as *Boxing News* stated, 'Cassius Clay burst upon London like a bomb. Whether for Cassius it will be the same as for Caesar, "Veni, vidi, vici", will not be resolved till 18 June, but without even bothering to look as far ahead the visit of Clay has been a shot in the arm for British boxing. Cassius, you're good for the game and we hope it'll be good for you.'

The following day was mundane in comparison: roadwork in Hyde Park at five a.m.; sparring in the Drill Hall of the 10th Parachute Battalion, TA, in Wood Lane, White City; a trip to Nottingham for the British middleweight title fight between George Aldridge and Mick Leahy. On Wednesday morning his sparring was interrupted by Nigeria's Minister of Labour and Sport, Chief J.H. Johnson; in the afternoon he went to Epsom and saw Relko win the Derby. The main event of the evening was a date with David Coleman in the *Sportsview* studio.

Although Peter Dimmock had an action-packed programme to present – the Derby, the England-Czechoslovakia soccer international and that middleweight title fight – we really only tuned in for the one item. This was as close as most of us were ever going to get to Cassius Marcellus Clay. Dimmock recalls the moment: 'We arranged the interview because he was a very hot property and way ahead of his time in terms of hype. *Sportsview* had a huge audience and he'd receive huge publicity; he was paid only a small fee. We had discussions with Paul Fox to decide upon questions but Clay had no prior knowledge of them because interviews became terribly stilted in those circumstances: we wanted to avoid that on live television;

Cassius Clay

Form No. 4

British Boxing Board of Control (1929)

RAMILLIES BUILDINGS, HILLS PLACE, LONDON, W.1

(Official Use only)

BOXER

APPLICATION FOR LICENCE

Fee: £1 per Annum

Received _12th June 1963_
Photos _"_
Medical Forms Rec'd _—_
Passed by A. M. O. _—_
Approved by A.B.A. _—_
Rec. By No.: _—_ Area Council
Date of Meeting _—_
Sig. of Secretary _—_
Date of Issue _1. 6. 63_
Granted by Board _12. 6. 63_
Head Office Record _√ one_
Licence No. _78781_
Reg. No. _B 1834G_
Entered _√ A_

Received by Area Council Sec.

Banked by Head Office:
13 JUN 1963
Head Office Receipt sent

Name in full { Professional _Cassius Clay_
{ Private _Cassius Marcellus Clay_

Address _7307 Virginia Way_
Louisville, Kentucky

Name of any amateur boxing clubs of which a member _—_

Amateur classification: Open/Inter/Novice (delete as applicable)

Age _21_ Date of Birth _Jan. 7/42_ Place of Birth _Louisville Ky_ Nationality _American_

Exact Boxing Weight at the time of application for Licence } _Hvy._

Number of Contests taken part in } Amateur _106_ Professional _19_

Name of Proposed Manager _Bill Faversham_

I hereby apply for a Licence as a Boxer and if this Licence is granted me I declare to adhere strictly to the Rules of The British Boxing Board of Control (1929) as printed, and abide by any further Rules or alteration to existing Rules as may be passed. I agree to pay the Fee in accordance with the above.

Date _12th June 1963_   Signed _Cassius M. Clay_

Witness _R. Blane_

Address _—_

(Two Passport Photographs, full face without a hat, must accompany this application)
MUST BE WRITTEN IN INK

you couldn't let things look rehearsed. We were always trying to find stories for the next day's papers, to beat them to it!'

The interview followed the customary pattern to begin with: the snazzily dressed (bow-tied, no less) young American cruising to a points victory. 'Ah'm gonna make the referee's job easy by kayoing Cooper. If Cooper whups me I'll get down on my hands and knees, crawl across the ring and kiss his feet. And then I'll take the next jet out of the country and I will be wearing a false moustache and beard.' This last remark was a reference to the disguise Floyd Patterson adopted when fleeing the auditorium after losing his world heavyweight title to Sonny Liston. The new champion, a massive, brooding, menacing ex-convict, was never far from Clay's thoughts now that he was the number-two contender (after Patterson) for the title. 'I'm only here to mark time before I annihilate that big, ugly bear,' he continued. 'I can draw them in no matter who I'm with. But there won't be no fight unless I get my cut. They have been paying the challenger nothing. I've talked up the greatest fight in history. Man, I don't need Liston. He needs ME! That big, ugly bear will take Patterson in three and when I meet Liston he'll fall in eight. He's too ugly to be a fighter. Real fighters are pretty like me!' Coleman pressed on: what about the threat posed by 'Enery's 'Ammer, the Englishman's famed left hook? 'Ah'm so fast I can turn out the light and be in bed before it's dark! Hittin' hard don't mean nothin' if you don't find nothin' to hit! There are two greats: Britain and CLAY!'

Then Coleman put his foot in it: 'I'm a Cooper fan and I know most British people are . . .' he got as far as saying, before the frosty stare from the seat opposite cut him short. 'I thought you were for me! I didn't have to come here, you know,' Coleman and a million viewers heard Cassius bark. ' I should be in bed right now! I'm going!' Thumping the arms of his chair he got up and stalked off the set. Coleman sat still, mortified. 'He really has gone,' confirmed an incredulous Dimmock. The interview had lasted eight minutes. But what an eight minutes! This was live television at its liveliest. Ace reporter Coleman and the clipped-voiced, trim-moustachioed Dimmock represented the older generation, the establishment. You couldn't treat them like that, could you? 'It was no stunt,' Cassius informed inquisitive hacks. 'I was very upset. What annoyed me was when the interviewer David Coleman said he was a Cooper fan and then said I talked too much. I shan't appear on radio or television again unless the interviewer is neutral and polite.'

Dimmock was taken completely unawares. 'Nothing ever surprised me about boxing but this was totally unexpected. We believed we were fairly hot stuff on news items but we had to retain our integrity and never went to great lengths to provoke a reaction in order to create news. Clay was a very amusing and intelligent chap to talk to, extremely articulate. I think he

More fool those who didn't believe him (Sport & General)

19

knew exactly what he was doing and there was no question in his mind: he was going to walk out! I've met him many times subsequently and we have laughed about that interview. He is far too intelligent to admit it was deliberate – even if he did plan it! For all I know it may have been spontaneous!'

In the wake of this perceived public display of bad manners the press felt able to go for the jugular. 'Keep talking Cass the Gas – you're doing a grand job for our 'Enery,' wrote the *Mirror*'s John Bromley. 'The more you babble away about being the greatest, the more you slam Cooper as a bum, the more our 'Enery likes it. Cooper has only to land a punch on Clay and the cheering will break out.' A letter from W.S. Jeanes of Littlestone in Kent seemed to summarise the growing mood of jingoism: 'Who is this obnoxious Cassius Clay? And why is he permitted to invade our shores with his nonsensical claptrap? A Churchillian salute to him to make him a loser in the second round against Henry Cooper.' *Boxing News* also made no bones about it: 'Henry Cooper will be doing millions of fight fans the world over a big favour if he manages to halt the upward trend of big-talking Clay. The Louisville Lip has, with his pathetic poetry and degrading insults to the British champ, turned everybody into a Cooper fan.' The paper even went so far as to devote a whole page to a collection of poetic vitriol from outraged readers, including one from Cooper's assistant trainer Victor George:

> *'We Britishers, being a tolerant race, welcome you Cassius Clay,*
> *In the manner of your compatriots Dwight Eisenhower, Billy Graham and*
>   *Danny Kaye.*
> *Yes, many Yanks have been feted inside old England's shores,*
> *Some have served most equitably, others like Perfect Bores.*
> *And, be what you may, dear Cassius Clay, you are welcome to our community,*
> *But be warned in time by this Master of rhyme,*
> *Our 'Enery's ATOM-BOMB conceals NO immunity.'*

Our 'Enery had the last word: 'Surely by now he knows that everyone in Britain hates his guts.'

However unintentionally, Cooper had squirted a decent jet of oil on to the cogs of the publicity machine. The young American braggart pitted against the 29-year-old elder statesman of British boxing represented the sound of rustling banknotes to Jack Solomons. And, it must be said, Cooper who, although not on a percentage of the actual gate, was on a percentage of the ancillary rights from television and cinema: the more people who became interested the better it was going to be. Cassius had got the message – as evidenced by a widely printed photo of him sporting a tape over his mouth, complete with padlock! On completion of his 96th and last round of sparring at White City he confined himself to saying: 'I'm a mean man, rarin' to go.' Down at the Fellowship Inn, a large pub in Bellingham where Cooper had his training camp, his opponent was no less reticent: 'I am confident I can beat Clay. That's all I want to say. Boxing is a funny business and it doesn't do to shoot off your mouth too much.' With that he went off to celebrate mass.

Cooper's strategy was simple enough: get Clay to back-pedal, trap him on the ropes – preferably in a corner – and unload the 'Ammer. According to scientists, who had studied its delivery via slow-motion photography, Cooper's left hook accelerated to 60 times the force of gravity in travelling five and a half inches; its speed on impact was 30 m.p.h.! This was Cooper's Sunday-punch, a potential saviour. The only problem was landing it. As he recalls: 'We knew he was out of the ordinary from the Olympics and what we'd read about him. He had this unconventional style with his arms down etc., but he had the speed and reflexes to get away with it. He was always on the move, never a sitting target. He was completely unorthodox and people couldn't manage to hit him. Others tried to copy him later on and got clobbered. There was only one original! His style unsettled bigger guys but lighter guys gave him greater trouble. You see, Doug Jones nearly beat him.'

As the hours of 18 June ticked away the task confronting Cooper grew no less daunting. 'The ageing hunter should not chase young tigers,' warned George Whiting of the *Evening Standard*. 'It must be Cassius – he may have difficulty in making it last five rounds,' insisted Peter Wilson. However, he offered Cooper one glimmer of hope: Clay, he observed, tends to sway back from a hook instead of stepping inside; if Cooper steps in quickly after a break Clay might sway right into the arc of another hook. For its part *Boxing News* was forced to confess: 'Clay just bamboozles and mesmerises opponents until they succumb to the quantity – not quality – of his punches.' Yes, what damage might Clay inflict with an advantage of 21 lbs in weight and two inches in reach? After all, he'd already stopped 14 of his 18 opponents. *The Times* suggested: 'His cutting left jab – and it is one of his faults that he tends to slash rather than punch with the full weight of his body – could mean real trouble for the fragile skin by Cooper's eyebrows.' It could not pass unnoticed that Cooper was invariably cut during his fights and had twice been stopped on cut eyes. A hard look, said one wag, was enough to start them bleeding; Reg Gutteridge joked, 'Even his potatoes get cut eyes.' Wilson concurred, though he waxed more lyrically: 'The leather-clad fists of Clay which fly as fast as swallows diving over the eaves of a house, will rip and score the tissue-paper-thin skin round Cooper's eyes.' In Cooper's most recent contest, Dick Richardson had split his eyebrow in the opening round but a barrage of left hooks in round five still yielded Cooper his fourth knockout in 27 victories.

The weigh-in (Cooper a very light, even for him, 13st 3½lbs; Clay 14st 11lbs) took place, appropriately enough, at the London Palladium. Boxing's brash new showman swung into action. Cassius spotted a cardboard crown left over from some pantomime or other and promptly stuck it on his head. 'You gotta Queen, you need a King!' he proclaimed. 'Ah am KING!'

More fool those who didn't believe him.

'ENERY'S 'AMMER

Wembley Stadium had not hosted a prize fight for 28 years; not since Jack Peterson defeated Walter Neusel in 1935. Solomons, with Clay's help, was confident of enticing 55,000 customers through the turnstiles. Nearly every one of them would be noisily spurring Cooper on, imploring him to button Clay's arrogant lip with the 'Ammer. It was, after all, the anniversary of Waterloo when England's 'Iron Duke' Wellington gave 'Boney' a bloody nose in 1815. Cassius would barely have a friend in the stadium. Sympathy came from an unlikely source. Peter Wilson was moved to say: 'In some way I am quite sorry for Clay, who is a victim of his own ticket-selling publicity. There won't be more than a handful of people hoping to see him win and yet this astonishing young negro has done more to restore worldwide interest in boxing than any individual I can remember since the palmiest days of Joe Louis.'

Britain's youth seldom gravitated towards 'live' boxing promotions; they could not afford the price of admission. Most of the six guineas seats had gone, Solomons was pleased to report. Clay's 11 millionaire backers, who had flown in by chartered jet (along with Angelo Dundee, fresh from supervising Rodriguez's victory over Griffiths) took 100 of them; other ringside seats would be occupied by the likes of Liz Taylor, Richard Burton and Shirley Bassey. However, plenty of the cheaper variety remained for those who were prepared to brave the stormy weather forecast and pay at the gate. When it came to controlling the elements for his outdoor shows Solomons was in the Cassius Clay league. Threatened with one rain-induced postponement he summoned journalists to his hotel 24 hours before the start of proceedings and pointed to a bucket he'd placed on the balcony. The astounded journos were informed that when the receptacle was full the rain would cease. The bucket filled, the rain stopped and the show went on as planned.

On this occasion the promoter received no help from the Almighty. Tuesday, 18 June, decided to be an exceedingly wet day. Spur-of-the-moment customers would be few and despite an undercard featuring Henry's twin, Jim, the visitor's sparring partners Ellis and Warner, plus a £500-to-the-winner tournament for heavyweights, the crowd was to fall way below expectations: 35,000 at most – some estimations put it as low as

*'You gotta Queen,
you need a King!'*

18,000. Nor had sales been boosted by the removal of the newly christened London Loudmouth from the front pages. Even Cass the Gas could not steal the thunder from Tory minister John Profumo, forced to resign in the wake of a sex scandal! With no live television coverage the only viable option for the multitude wishing to follow the fight as it happened was to tune the radio to the Light Programme at 9.15 p.m. and listen to the blow-by-blow commentary of Simon Smith, augmented by inter-round summaries by W. Barrington Dalby.

This was most definitely a case of the men of the house gathering round a transistor radio strategically placed on the kitchen table. Neither wives nor mothers nor daughters wanted anything to do with yet another skirmish in the traditional family feud involving male factions of disparate age and inclination. 'And now, over to Wembley where Simon Smith is your commentator for tonight's eagerly awaited heavyweight fight between British and Empire champion Henry Cooper and the former Olympic light-heavyweight champion Cassius Clay of the United States.' A fragile peace envelops the kitchen table. The decks are cleared for action; glasses and cups are pushed aside and cigarettes are lit to concentrate the mind. Heads tilt toward the radio, ears alert for the latest news and the sound of battle. Smith paints a word picture for us. Thankfully, the rain has abated and no longer threatens to ruin the spectacle for all those privileged celebrities at ringside (shame!). There's the fanfare from six scarlet-clad trumpeters of the Coldstream Guards. Here comes Clay, the spotlight just picking him out. Angelo Dundee precedes him into the ring and then Smith's words are drowned beneath a floodtide of whistles and catcalls from the partisan home crowd: to a man it has caught sight of the American's ensemble. He cuts a dashing figure, resplendent in a scarlet robe with white piping beneath which matching shorts and white boots can be distinguished – and, yes, he's wearing that crown. The arms are aloft, taped hands spread wide, as he strolls round the ring, affording each and every spectator full view of the legend emblazoned from shoulder to shoulder across his back: 'Cassius Clay, The Greatest'. The chorus of boos is building to yet another mighty crescendo when suddenly the opening blast of a second fanfare slams the door in its face. 'Enery is on his way! The tranquillity proves short-lived, exceedingly so, in fact. As Cooper makes his way to the ring from the opposite side of the arena the noise is cacophonous. In pubs, clubs and kitchens throughout the land final thoughts are aired, allegiances reaffirmed and predictions risked. 'SECONDS OUT!'

The exact events of the ensuing 17 minutes and 15 seconds lie buried among the rubble of personal recollection but their impact is indelibly recorded in the sporting memory bank of every man – young or old – who lived through them. In what seemed the blink of an eye we hear the roar of approval as the first of 'Enery's 'Ammers strikes home, drawing blood from Clay's nose. The American is angry, we are told, at Cooper's tactics of holding and hitting. His protests to referee Tommy Little fall on deaf ears: not surprising given the chants of 'Coo-per, Coo-per' rolling round the stadium! Cooper continues to rough Clay up as the bell brings a sensational first three minutes to an end. Round one to the older generation.

Round two, however, teaches fathers and elder brothers alike that it is unwise to crow. Cooper sustains a cut under the left eye, not too serious according to Smith but a sign that the left lead of Cassius is beginning to find rhythm and range. Round three brings more of the same and Smith's voice registers disappointment at the realisation that Cooper is now also cut over the left eye. No one needs to tell his opponent: he knows Cooper is in deep trouble. It is an opportunity for him to showboat. He starts to dance round the ring, hands down by his side, taunting Cooper. This is too much for British manhood to bear. Proud men of El Alamein vintage are baying for Clay's blood now; those of fresher complexion wisely try to conceal the 'I-told-you-so' smirks. We know Cassius will 'carry' 'Enery till the witching hour that is round five, don't we? Barrington Dalby hands back to Smith who reports hearing Bill Faversham, Clay's principal backer, calling over to Angelo Dundee: 'Tell him to cut out the funny business and get down to work!' The admonishment works. The jabs begin to pepper Cooper's eye once more. 'Pop! Pop! Pop! That's it!' an American voice can be heard shouting loud and clear. 'Pop! Pop! Pop!' It's just a matter of time now.

Then radios everywhere appear to explode; transistors jump off the tables; or they are knocked flying through the air. A sound akin to amplified gargling has replaced the commentary. To the boxing fan this means only one thing: someone is down and in this particular instance such tribal acclamation signifies it can only be Cassius Marcellus Clay. Smith confirms a left hook has put Clay on the canvas for a count of three just before the bell. Everyone is on their feet. Discarded chairs and stools litter floors. Smirks are summarily wiped from countless teenage faces by the repercussions of that single sweeping left-hand punch, more adroitly than any sternly delivered paternal back-hander. 'Thattaboy, 'Enery! Knock the shit out of him! Take his effing head off!' Fathers are suddenly in their element. 'What is all the racket?' enquire a million mothers round a million kitchen doors. 'And there's no call for that filthy language, either!'

That, mother, is debatable; highly debatable. Things are getting serious; not half as serious as things in the American corner, however. Tommy Little is being called over. Whatever for? Surely he's not going to stop the fight? No, the bell has sounded for round five and the only name on Smith's lips is Clay. Cassius is transformed into the devil incarnate; he is pouring punches on to Cooper's face and the left eye is soon a gory mess. Then it's

JACK SOLOMONS presents an

Eliminating Contest for the

HEAVYWEIGHT CHAMPIONSHIP OF THE WORLD

Wembley Stadium
Tuesday 18th June, 1963

OFFICIAL PROGRAMME TWO SHILLINGS & SIXPENCE

Cassius Clay

Henry Cooper

(Perry Aghajanoff Collection)

all over! Tommy Little is leading 'Enery towards his corner; a stunned commentator describes Clay strutting round the ring, ruler of all he surveys, victor in the fifth – just as he assured us he would be. Collapse of the old order: teenage sons one, fathers nil. The elder generation slinks away to sulk in its tent.

One advantage of being a paperboy on 19 June 1963 was the priceless opportunity to read all the fight coverage for free. Having selected a convenient wall to recline against, the contents of the paper-bag could be plundered at will. What did Peter Wilson have to say? Under the banner headline 'Clay wins in five with a "bare" fist', the characteristically purple prose of 'The Man they can't gag' talks of Cooper's hooks being like 'slicing sickles', his ultimate visage akin to a 'red-rimmed cyclops'; horsehair from Clay's torn glove and blood from Cooper's torn face, he tells us, splatters the very typewriter he is using to spread the news that, in his opinion, Cooper won all four completed rounds. 'Any suggestion that Clay – fast though he is, clever at blocking and swaying out of range – should be matched with Sonny Liston in the near future should be laughed out of the rings of the world.' In the *Daily Mail*, Harry Carpenter was no less forthright. 'Coming into the ring wearing that ridiculous crown many may think he is doing his best to cheapen the fight game. And I must agree. His performance was not all that great.' The same paper's trenchant columnist J.L. Manning roars: 'If this immature American boxer can be knocked down by a half-blind opponent with no reputation as a heavy puncher then he should be matched more moderately.' What did the boxing correspondent (no bylines in 1963) of *The Times* have to say? 'Feat of Clay: Wembley promise fulfilled' was the lead, but the conclusions were just the same: 'Bombast and fast reflexes are not enough to succeed in professional boxing'. However, there is something odd about the report. A second reading confirms it: there is no mention of a split glove.

The ensuing day and its quota of GCE exams could not pass soon enough for all us paperboys and other like-minded representatives of teenage Britain. Full coverage of the fight was promised in *Sportsview* at 8.20 p.m. Sorry, mum, it's your turn to inhabit the kitchen tonight. The television's tiny 14-inch screen is all the more minuscule thanks to the enormity of its cumbersome wooden casing. Cue Carpenter, Harry that is. Despite the far from perfect black-and-white images it proves impossible to find fault with his assessment of the young negro's physique. 'Clay really is a fine figure of a man,' he opines as Cassius disrobes. 'Shake hands and when the bell rings come out boxing, and may the best man win,' Tommy Little tells the two protagonists while Jim Wicks and Angelo Dundee attempt to peer over their respective shoulders. It is not difficult to see why Simon Smith quickly got so excited. Anyone ignorant of the eventual winner could have foreseen a knockout for Cooper. Throughout the

Coo-per! Coo-per!'
The British
champion stalks
his prey
(Popperfoto)

opening round the British champion stalks Clay remorselessly, thudding
left hooks into body and head. It is, indeed, largely one-way traffic and it is
Cooper, ironically, who inside a minute draws first blood, from Clay's nose.
'Cooper has hurt Clay, who is hanging on,' shouts Harry. 'He's blinking
and frowning. Cooper has certainly not started apprehensively tonight; the
man who has started so many fights too quietly has come out full of fight.
Clay argues with the referee that Cooper is trying to hold him – and he's
getting angry. At one stage there I thought he even poked his arm out at Mr
Tommy Little. This is a sensational fight! Clay has gone fighting mad!' Yes,
there's no question who is on top as the initial three minutes peter out. The
young upstart has been harried from pillar to post and bustled out of his
stride. Cooper's round by a mile. 'That has done wonders for British
professional boxing,' enthuses Carpenter. 'People are on their feet at the
ringside cheering Cooper . . . this is quite the most extraordinary fight night
I've ever experienced in Britain. Can Cooper beat Clay and put British
heavyweight boxing right on top of the heavyweight world?'

   In comparison with that all-action session the second round began
tamely. You could see Cooper was scoring with some half-decent left hooks,
and one huge ooh-inducing haymaker would have caused instant
decapitation had it connected, but by the same token Clay was clearly

beginning to string the jabs together. 'It's the Cooper left hook against the left jab of Clay and there's no telling at this stage which punch is going to come out on top,' confided Carpenter. Before he is given the opportunity of contemplating how fate has been well and truly tempted a dark smudge becomes visible beneath Cooper's left eye. Equally apparent are the two ramrodding straight lefts which graze the left side of 'Enery's face 40 seconds into the next round, leaving the eyebrow pouring blood. 'This is what we always feared. He's going to have a job to get through with that eye. Cooper's now fighting desperately because he knows his time may be short. There's no telling how long he's got to go with that eye!' You can recognise the selfsame conjecture written all over Clay's face as he breaks into a quickstep and turns the ring into a dance-floor. 'He's contemptuously treating Cooper,' wails Harry, 'just using his feet to keep away from Cooper. This is complete cheek on the part of Clay, who feels he's got it in the bag because of that eye. He's barely bothering to punch, he's just threatening and teasing Cooper, trying to make him look small.'

Precise knowledge as to when the 'Ammer declares itself during the fourth still fails to dull a keen sense of anticipation as the round starts. Not that we knew it but 'Enery was almost denied his greatest moment: Wicks had wanted to stop the fight there and then on account of the two-inch slit on Cooper's left eye. Cooper is already pawing at it like an injured animal in a vain attempt to staunch the flow of blood before the first punch comes across. Cassius is playing the young swell now. Off balance, he throws an extravagant right which whistles wide and nearly causes him to topple over. All the evidence points to the fact that he is going to carry Cooper until the appointed round. Once he really unleashes a series of combinations on the dark bullseye which doubles for Cooper's eye the contest must swiftly reach its denouement. Echoing Cooper's frustration, Carpenter laments: 'One looks for a sign that a left hook from Cooper could really hurt this man but apart from the opening minute he hasn't seemed to hurt Clay very much . . . but anything might happen.'

The 'Ammer strikes – indisputably the most famous photograph in British boxing history (Sport & General)

Harry is obviously working the oracle to a tee, one cannot avoid thinking, knowing the drama which is about to unfold. Cassius, facing the camera, is circling to his left, towards the ropes and away from Cooper's left-hand bombs, when one which seems to originate from the bowels of the camera detonates on the side of his chin. There's no mistaking that expression of pain and confusion as his backside thuds on to the canvas via the bottom rope. He's up at a count of three no one can hear above the bedlam and it's only thanks to Carpenter that we know the bell has sounded to end the round. Years later Cooper recalled: 'The ropes helped make the situation but they also saved him. If I'd caught him in the centre of the ring there would have been nothing to break his fall and it's the fall on the canvas that shakes you up as much as the punch. And he should

have stayed down for as long as possible. For him to get up like that was a classic boxing error which he was lucky to get away with: it's the kind of mistake a novicey guy makes. He wanted to prove he hadn't been hurt but he walked back to his corner like a drunk. If it had all happened in the middle of the round he would have jumped up just the same and I'd have finished him off. I was in my prime then and I didn't let them off the hook once they were groggy.'

Cassius tottered towards the healing arms of Angelo Dundee like an errant tippler. Dundee plonked him on the stool and got to work. From beyond the ropes Dick Reekie, Dundee's English agent and cornerman, can be seen massaging Clay's shoulders, while Chickie Ferrara breaks a vital phial of smelling-salts under his nostrils. 'And he still doesn't know where he is!' bellows Carpenter. 'They're working furiously on him . . . and Angelo Dundee really is giving him a talking-to!' Of course, Angelo was doing a lot more than just talking: as he subsequently confessed, he was aggravating a split on his fighter's left glove in order to prolong his recovery time. Not even the prying eye of television can spot the chicanery, however, because of the wall of white jackets screening the corner. Over comes referee Little – apart from his black bow-tie, also clad in white from head to toe – to further obscure proceedings, but it is obvious something is afoot even before Carpenter mentions it in commentary: 'I think Clay has got a torn glove!' Cooper's cut-man, Danny Holland, looks toward the timekeeper and points at his own wristwatch. 'Seconds out!' Clang! Clang! The interval is 65 seconds, not the prescribed 60: so, no big deal there.

It is a totally different Cassius Clay we are seeing now, something for which those measly extra seconds and the smelling-salts cannot entirely be responsible. Pride has been dented and, after all, this is round five. Clay hounds his quarry and within 20 seconds hurls a crunching short right over the top of Cooper's guard which lands right on the damaged eye. Cooper winces at impact. His face and chest are running with blood and it is noticeable that each subsequent blow from Clay's left hand causes a tuft of horsehair to be ejected like a spent cartridge. 'Oh! Now Cooper's left eye really is in a shocking state,' cries Carpenter. 'It's the worst cut eye I've seen for a very, very long time indeed. I do not see how Tommy Little can let this go much further.' At ringside Liz Taylor is also screaming at the top of her not inconsiderable voice for the fight to be stopped. Said Cooper afterwards: 'You don't actually feel a bad cut. It just stings and goes numb. What tells you it's a bad one is when you feel the warm blood dripping on your body. This one felt just like a tap pouring on my chest.' Little calls a halt with one minute ten seconds on the clock, just as the towel is thrown in. Clay commences his second walkabout of the night, arms aloft, before leaning over the ropes and holding up the right glove: 'I told you five!' For his pains he receives a barrage of boos and a salvo of programmes.

The towel barely disguises a 'red-rimmed cyclops' (Sport & General)

Henry Cooper, to this day, bears no grudge. 'The boxing public generally are a bloodthirsty lot. They like to see a good hard fight and if there's plenty of gore and snot flying around they love it. Years later Ali told me that the left hook I caught him with was the hardest he ever took. He said it hurt him so much that it not only shook him but his ancestors in Africa as well!' The victor felt obliged to swallow some humble pie: 'I underestimated him. His left hook was good. Cooper shook me up. He hit me harder than I've ever been hit. I've been on the floor before but not hurt so much. Cooper is a real fighter. Cooper was great, the toughest nut yet. He is no longer a bum. The booing didn't shock me. I'm always booed!'

The press continued – naturally – to extract mileage from the controversy surrounding the split glove. 'It was a "natural" break,' declared Thursday's *Daily Mirror* after interviewing relevant parties. Tommy Little was quoted thus: 'As far as I know the glove was all right between the third and fourth rounds or else my attention would have been drawn to it. I was told about it at the end of the fourth and ordered a new pair to be brought and used in the sixth.' BBBC secretary Teddy Waltham had this to say: 'I have examined the glove and I am satisfied it was a natural split down the seam.' Lastly, Jim Wicks had his tuppenceworth: 'I saw the glove was split in the interval after the fourth but thought it better

33

to get the fight going again as quickly as possible. I could have let them wait to get a new glove but a delay would have been of much more advantage to Clay than us.' Reg Gutteridge also examined the damaged glove. 'The tear was at the base of the thumb and so it was impossible for his knuckles to have bared in the way some people said. I was seated in the front row facing the royal box and in front of the late Andy Cunningham, chief inspector of the BBBC, and the secretary, Teddy Waltham. They had a quick discussion before the finish of the third round and Cunningham, or it might have been Harry Vines, rushed to find a replacement glove. It was delivered to Ali's corner before the end of the fourth, although there was no instruction for the glove to be changed until the referee ordered it. And another thing I'd like to say is that he refused to wear that crown after the fight. Someone tried to put it on him but he pushed it away. He didn't want to make sport after cutting someone up like that.'

It only remained for Friday's *Boxing News* to tie up the loose ends. Amid all the expert analysis, however, two readers' letters perhaps caught the moment. 'The Gas Bag from Louisville didn't beat Cooper; it was old Mother Nature,' said Billy Jones of Downham, in Kent. By contrast, Dennis Rickman, of Fowey in Cornwall, gave some praise and a little advice to the victor: 'Cassius – you have done boxing the world over a fantastic amount of good and I for one am *certain* that you are not the brash, bighead you would have us believe. Good luck in the future but *please* keep your hands up or you will never be world champion.'

Cassius had no opportunity to read either letter as he was already on his way back to America, his armour of self-belief perfectly intact. His British adventure was summarised thus: 'I'll demolish Sonny Liston in eight rounds and he'll be in a worse fix if I predict six! I'll fight Liston if the price is right. If Telstar is working a Clay-Liston fight would draw a $100 million gate. I'm very big in those foreign countries. They love me over there!'

THE TECHNICOLOR BROTHER

Paddy Monaghan takes his campaign on to the streets (Paddy Monaghan Collection)

Paddy Monaghan has been called Muhammad Ali's biggest fan. He is that, and more: he is a friend. Indeed, Ali refers to him as his Technicolor Brother. This friendship, cemented by regular visits to each other's homes over a period of 30 years, began with a bizarre exchange on a London pavement in June 1963. 'Who'd have thought then, when I was just a wide-eyed kid who thought it was great to shake the guy's hand, that we'd become the close friends we are now.'

Once encountered in the flesh, the seemingly implausible notion that an illiterate hod-carrier from, as he puts it, 'out in the sticks', could forge an undying relationship with boxing's most famous figure no longer surprises. A body all whipcord and wire, the bristling moustache and that growl of a voice spell out F-I-G-H-T-E-R in capital letters far larger than the slight, boyish frame might otherwise have suggested. Even two heart attacks have failed to stem the tremendous drive oozing from every pore. Such vitality spurred Monaghan to teach himself to read and write after he left school where, yes, he was by his own admission 'a bit of a scrapper – you had to be if you were from Ireland in those days'.

Lacking sufficient finesse to succeed under the Marquess of Queensberry rules as an amateur – a handful of bouts at welterweight – he drew on all his native pluck to earn some much-needed cash 'on the cobbles' as a street-fighter. This indomitable spirit also fuelled the one-man campaign he waged against the world boxing authorities for stripping Ali of his title which not only attracted 22,224 signatories and grew into the Muhammad Ali Fan Club but also brought him to the attention of Ali himself. Paddy Monaghan is Muhammad Ali's kind of guy: what you see is what you get.

'It all started in 1963 really. I took the day off work – I was hod-carrying at the time – to go and see him train before the first Cooper fight. I'd followed him since the Olympics and seen the Miteff and Lavorante fights on TV; I thought I'd seen a future world champion. I'd always been a great lover of boxing and what attracted me to him was that everyone was saying he did everything wrong, what with his hands down by his sides and his chin stuck out. Well, it turned out that everything he was doing wrong he was doing right. He was training at the TA Centre in Wood Lane, Shepherds Bush, but I was given the wrong time and arrived an hour late. As I got there crowds were outside the door. Muhammad, Clay as he was then, came out – I could see him head and shoulders above the crowd even though I was stood way back on the other side of the road – and he's still shaking hands with all and sundry. I thought to myself, "This is no act". There were no TV cameras around; he wasn't like some politician who only does this kind of thing if the cameras are there. That instantly made me take to him.'

It is not difficult to imagine the feelings of the young Monaghan left cursing his luck on the opposite pavement: so near yet so far. Then the inexplicable happened. 'To my amazement he walked through the crowd over to me, standing alone on the other side of the road, and put out his hand. "How ya doin? Where ya bin?" He thought he knew me. "Where have we met before?" Looking back I've got to pinch myself to believe it all happened. My mates all asked: "Where's his autograph?" but I was so over-whelmed at the time I'd completely flipped and forgot to ask for it.'

After this initial, extraordinary tête-à-tête Paddy Monaghan's relation-ship with the charismatic young heavyweight contender immediately reverted to the level of everyone else: he admired from afar. But the strength of his admiration was soon put to the test, at Wembley on 18 June. 'I was about the only Clay supporter in the stadium,' he recalls ruefully. 'I think I had to fight harder than Muhammad. I got in a dust-up with a few

MUHAMMAD ALI
MONTHLY

NUMBER ONE   FEBRUARY *1972.

Our Champ

(Paddy Monaghan Collection)

others who were waving Union Jacks and shouting for Cooper.'

Local differences of opinion – albeit thankfully less physical in character – regarding the outcome of the world championship bout with Sonny Liston were almost as fraught for the challenger's solitary Abingdon supporter. 'Liston was a big favourite and I was the only one round here who said Muhammad would beat him. They were paying too much attention to the papers but I was paying attention to Muhammad's boxing skills. My mother stood by me but my brothers said Liston would knock him out in a round. Muhammad's victory meant a lot to me because my friends had been so insistent. I can remember now lying in bed early in the morning listening to the fight on the radio and letting out a big yell when he won.'

Tiny spats like the aforementioned are food and drink to any devoted fan. Something far more serious was brewing and Paddy Monaghan's reaction to it would lift him from the serried ranks of Ali fans to the elevated position of Ali confidant. For Ali's friendship Monaghan owes a vote of thanks to the world boxing authorities who stripped the champion of his title on 28 April 1967. Monaghan was beside himself with fury.

'How could they do that for actions outside the ring? They'd robbed him of his constitutional rights. Who the hell were the boxing authorities to act as judge and jury by taking his licence away? He was on bail pending appeal. He'd had his passport withheld but he should have been allowed to box anywhere in the USA. Something had to be done, I told myself. But it was crazy, really. What could one man – a hod-carrier from a little place like Abingdon – do to make the world boxing authorities sit up and take notice? What could I do to bring this situation to the eyes of the world? Sweet FA!'

Nevertheless, as the tormented hod-carrier paced his living-room floor deep into the night a fighting policy slowly crystallised: get other like-minded individuals to express their displeasure. This was, after all, 1967; organise a petition; demonstrate. So Paddy Monaghan took his fight onto the streets, more specifically to Park Lane and the very portals of the American Embassy.

'I made a banner, "Ali is our Champ" it said, hung between two broom handles which I held up in front of me as I walked. On my back I had a board with the petition on it and a pen hanging down for people to sign with. Up and down Park Lane I went like that for the three and a half years Muhammad was out of the ring. The first time I got arrested as I didn't have a police permit. I didn't know all demonstrations had to have one. The second time I wrote off for one and had a couple of policemen on either side of me. By the time I reached Speaker's Corner I had a mass of people behind me chanting "Ali! Ali! Ali!" and they even passed the banner round to give me a rest. Then I'd start to speak – next to Lord Soper, I remember.

Ali hugs his 'Technicolor Brother' on a visit to Monaghan's Abingdon home (Paddy Monaghan Collection)

I'm not academically gifted; I couldn't read or write when I left school at the age of 15 and taught myself to read using Enid Blyton books; I'm no orator, either. But I didn't need to be a brain surgeon to understand that what the authorities had done was wrong. If I – an ordinary guy – could understand it, anyone could. I called Ali "The People's Champion", a title no one had ever used or heard of before.'

Paddy Monaghan's indefatigable cause struck a chord with the sporting public and instantly caught fire. His activities provided plentiful copy for the local Oxford press and the odd inch or two for the nationals. Letters began arriving from Europe and all over the world; colleges and universities offered to collect names for the 'Ali is our Champ' petition on his behalf. 'I'd receive boxes of mail from everywhere, countries I'd never even heard of. In those three and a half years I got 22,224 names and addresses, which is how the fan club was formed.'

The world boxing authorities were not the only organisation to feel Monaghan's wrath. Armed with his trusty suitcase full of names and addresses he marched into the American Embassy demanding to see the ambassador himself: he wanted the names passed to President Nixon. Despite the heavy hand of the military promptly announcing its presence an attaché listened 'very cordially and politely' and gave his assurance the petition would find its way before the President.

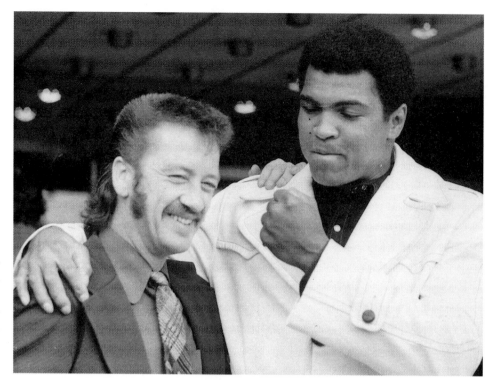

October 1971. Eight years after their first encounter, Monaghan and Ali are reunited (Paddy Monaghan Collection)

To the list of powerful bodies – World Boxing Council, New York State Athletic Commission, United States Government – which he had confronted in Ali's cause Monaghan eventually added possibly the most powerful and dangerous body of them all: Joe Frazier's. The new heavyweight champion of the world was not renowned for being an easy-going, laid-back sort of chap. His temper was of the hair-trigger variety and it is surely not too far-fetched to say that Monaghan took his life in his hands when he decided to confront Smokin' Joe at Heathrow Airport on 14 June 1971.

'I'd become a figurehead for Ali's fans worldwide, a spokesman, and all of them wanted to say to Joe Frazier: "Hey, Ali is our Champ. You're the Establishment's Champ." The job was mine, I had to do it. If I didn't do it I'd be letting the fans down. I expected it of myself. He was coming over here with his pop group The Knock-Outs, so I went to the airport to meet him. As he came through customs I unravelled the banner: "Ali is our Champ". He went berserk. His hand luggage went flying across the terminal. "What the f***'s this?" I'd really got him mad; he was fuming. As he was the world heavyweight champion I hoped he'd remember how to restrain himself when faced with someone like me. He didn't. He didn't hit me but he came near it. I'd rehearsed my speech:"Go back home! You're Howard Hughes's Champ; Richard Nixon's Champ! But Muhammad Ali is our Champ!" Everything went quiet. Even the security stood back. Frazier stuck his head down so his forehead touched mine and he was saying: "Put that thing down, you f****** bastard. I'll f****** kill you." I just kept repeating "Ali is our Champ" but I thought if I see any sign of a punch he'll get these two broom handles across his head which would stall him enough for me to make a dive out of the way. All of a sudden I felt my legs being kicked and punched: it was his pop group. They'd jumped me. I remember dropping a couple of them before airport police held me and all sorts of people were restraining Joe Frazier. "You're Drop-Outs not Knock-Outs," I shouted at them.' Two years later Monaghan gave the new 'champion' George Foreman exactly the same treatment outside the Connaught Rooms when he came to London.

News of his British ally's exploits gradually trickled through to the People's Champion, although he was uncertain what to make of such an unlikely story. Any reservations were dispelled, however, once his manager Herbert Muhammad had visited London earlier in 1971. Sitting in his room at the Royal Lancaster Hotel one day he was informed that a gentleman carrying a large black bag was in the lobby asking to meet him: Paddy

Now it's George Foreman's turn to face the music (Paddy Monaghan Collection)

From Madison Square Garden to Monaghan's Back Garden: Ali dons gloves to spar with Monaghan's son, Tyrone (Paddy Monaghan Collection)

Monaghan had struck again. 'I must have looked like Crocodile Dundee going into the hotel with this bag over my shoulder. Herbert Muhammad dug into the mail and read some to see if all that he and Ali had heard was genuine. Then he promised that the next time Muhammad came to England he'd write and let me know.' A few weeks later Monaghan received a letter from the States. 'Memo from Muhammad Ali', the top left-hand corner stated; underneath it said: 'Thank you, Paddy. Keep up the good work. Look forward to seeing you.'

That meeting came on 11 October 1971, a year after Ali had regained both his passport and the right to box. In between facing Messrs Ellis and Mathis he made a trip to Britain to endorse a new Ovaltine drink. To his legion of fans it was a heaven-sent opportunity to roll out the red carpet and pay homage. Paddy Monaghan decided to do the job properly or not at all. Accompanied by a strip of regally coloured carpet he once more headed for Heathrow – albeit with a far more pleasant confrontation in mind. As Ali strolled out to a typically raucous welcome Monaghan unrolled the carpet at his feet. 'A big smile came over his face and his eyes opened wide. He turned back, walked down the red carpet and put out his hand. I told him my name and he said he'd heard of me and what I'd been doing.'

Thus, eight years after that incredulous encounter in Wood Lane this second handshake signified the onset of a friendship the like of which Monaghan never visualised in his wildest dreams. Instead of a polite 'Goodbye' Ali put his arm round Monaghan and said: 'You tag along with me.' During the ensuing 60 minutes Monaghan saw the inside of the VIP lounge, a Rolls-Royce and a plush hotel suite. 'It was like another world. I didn't know what was going on.'

The following year Monaghan journeyed to Ali's Cherry Hill home in New Jersey and in November 1974 Ali made the first of his nine visits to Abingdon. 'We've had to clear a path for him sometimes when the news has got out that he's coming here. I've had my fence broken and a windowpane cracked by people trying to get a closer look.' In all honesty Monaghan became quite a local celebrity – a status he soon began to appreciate as something of a mixed blessing.

He started a boxing club in Abingdon and, thanks to all his publicity, donations and offers of equipment proved numerous; by the same token so were the entrepreneurs who sought to exploit this personal route to Ali in search of a fast buck. More hurtful is the recurring charge that Ali and hangers-on have become synonymous: is Monaghan just another one of them? 'I've never been on the "ear'ole" with Muhammad. Apart from that first trip to America I've always paid my own fare; I never go unless I can pay my way. At the same time I know I've only got to lift the phone and say I'd like to come over and the ticket would be waiting. It was the same for all Muhammad's fights. He'd say: "You never ask me for nothing. You can come to any of my fights." And I've been approached by all sorts of businessmen with various deals but I have had nothing to do with them.'

After the first Cooper fight Monaghan, in fact, only saw Ali perform in the flesh twice more. Al 'Blue' Lewis in Dublin and the second Frazier fight in New York. Being Paddy Monaghan, however, brought some compensations – notably the best seat in the house. For both these contests he was in Ali's corner.

'I'd travelled America with Ali in 1972 working in his corner for several exhibitions but at that time I was unlicensed – I'm a licensed trainer now – and because of that the Irish Boxing Board of Control was adamant I couldn't be in Muhammad's corner for the Lewis fight. Well, Muhammad was equally adamant I was going to be in his corner. This started a bit of a ruckus. We were all staying at the Opperman Hotel in the Wicklow Mountains and Hal Conrad, the co-promoter who was shaking like a leaf because of his investment in the fight, came to me with an open cheque in an effort to resolve the situation. "Name your price. Give Muhammad a reason why you're not going to be in his corner," he said. "No, I can't lie to the man," I replied. The argument got more heated as the days passed and I got so fed up with it that at one meeting I stood up and said: "I'm sick of listening to all this. I'll not be in the corner." One of the Board officials got up, clapped his hands and said: "Good. That's settled then." Muhammad just sat there, looking at me, and then he slowly raises his hand: "He's in my corner." The Board had to give way and on the day of the fight Hal Conrad came running to me carrying my licence. "Hang on to it, that'll be worth something one day. It's the most unusual licence you'll ever see." On it were the words to effect: "For Paddy Monaghan, c/o Muhammad Ali-'Blue' Lewis show, Croke Park. For one show only." I had no official role whatsoever, I didn't even hold a bucket, but I was allowed to climb into the ring before the fight and be with Muhammad, which was a magic moment.'

Eighteen months later Monaghan enjoyed the experience, priceless for a fight fanatic, of being in Ali's corner at one of boxing's legendary venues: Madison Square Garden, boxing's very own Mecca. 'When he was due to fight Frazier for the second time an air charter company wrote to me asking for a list of the fan club members and in return I'd get a free ticket and hotel room. I told them I'd not need a ticket to the fight, just give me the flight and room. I went to the Garden in a stretch limo as a member of Muhammad's entourage. It was crazy. Crowds were jumping on the bonnet and Ali had the window down and is waving to them. Anyway, to reach the ring we had to go down this big, long corridor which was lined with cops. Everyone had to have caps and badges to signify they were members of the entourage and I'd not got any. Suddenly I feel a hand on my shoulder and a bloody great cop is about to frogmarch me away. I shouted for Muhammad and he comes back. This was the nearest thing I've seen to him being in a temper. "Get your hands off him," he says through clenched teeth and the cop let me go.'

All three Ali-Frazier fights were classics but Monaghan has further reason to treasure memories of their Madison Square Garden clash in January 1974. Mindful of those sterling services rendered at Heathrow in the teeth of a Joe Frazier temper-tantrum Ali had whispered to his pal: 'This is one for you, Paddy.' Not that Monaghan was out of the woods as far as tangling with Smokin' Joe was concerned. The two men were to come eyeball to eyeball at the post-fight press conference.

'When we arrived for Ali's conference Frazier was still there because he'd turned up late for his. He was a helluva mess, he looked as though he'd been through a meat grinder; and Muhammad is in a pinstripe suit looking like a businessman. I stood by the bottom of the stage and I can see Frazier lifting up his dark glasses and staring down at me through these slits. I thought: "Shit, he remembers me from the airport." Under the stage I spot a piece of wood, so I get my foot on it ready in case he goes for me. When he had finished his spot he comes across and says: "Don't I know you? Where you from? What's your name?"' Monaghan looked the

Grosvenor House Hotel, 12 August 1977: Ali throws a party in honour of Sandra and Paddy Monaghan (Paddy Monaghan Collection)

battered Frazier in the eye and in the best antipodean accent he could muster replied: 'No, mate. My name's Bruce and I come from Australia.'

Although the Ali-Monaghan tandem never again operated at close quarters on a fight night, Ali was not one to shun any opportunity of reinforcing their special relationship. 'I was sitting in this cinema watching the Bob Foster fight on closed-circuit from Nevada and at the end of the post-fight interview Muhammad says: "I want to say hello to my friend over in England, Paddy Monaghan." I felt like nudging all the people around me and saying: "Hey, that's me!" And he did the same on *Sports Review of the Year* one time. Princess Anne was making the presentations and when Harry Carpenter began his satellite link with Muhammad he told him about her being in the studio. So Muhammad says: "Hello, Princess! And I want to say hello to my friend Paddy Monaghan as well." I'm just sat there watching TV at home and can't believe it. Friends started knocking on the door and ringing up to ask: "Did you see the programme? Did you see it?"' Topping even this recurring accolade was the Grand Testimonial Reception and Dinner at the Grosvenor House Hotel which Ali threw in Monaghan's honour on 12 August 1977.

Monaghan's voice still rises at the recollection of yet another barely credible milestone along the road to blood-brotherhood he and Ali have journeyed since that fleeting introductory handshake of 1963. 'If I could have saved all the money I've put into the fan club and the campaign over the years I'd be a lot better off. But I wouldn't change a thing. The first message I got when I was in hospital after this latest heart attack was from Muhammad and Lonnie. You can't buy that; that's the only reward I want.'

'MAN, I COULD HEAR HIM BLEEDING'

The newest and brightest star in boxing's firmament illuminated British skies once again during the summer of 1966. However, the returning comet was not quite the incandescent shooting-star of 1963. Much of the glow remained but some of the trailing sparks had gone. The Cassius Clay in blind pursuit of his fistic destiny no longer existed. That Cassius Clay had captured the heavyweight championship of the world. But he was no more. In his stead walked Muhammad Ali, an altogether greater manifestation.

Despite ruefully accepting the former state of affairs, the British press was not yet ready to swallow the latter: it insisted on addressing the new champion as Cassius Clay even though two years had elapsed since his change of name on becoming a Muslim. Ali's links with the Nation of Islam – an organisation widely regarded to be more political than religious – and his subsequent request for military service deferment were sensitive issues. With its young men dying by the thousand in the jungles of Vietnam and its streets bursting with evidence of racial tension, America – mainstream America – was becoming weary of the 'uppity nigger'. When he dismissed the establishment's next challenger, Floyd Patterson, who had announced his intention to 'reclaim the title for America', as being nothing more than an 'Uncle Tom', the writing was on the wall. Once Ali had toyed with the former champion, both physically and psychologically, for 12 painful rounds in February 1965, boxing's power-brokers began reaching for sledgehammers to knock the wall down. Illinois and Ali's home state of Kentucky were among those who refused to stage the next planned defence against Ernie Terrell. Political pressure saw the fight eventually switched to Toronto, by which time Terrell had backed out. Local heavy George Chuvalo willingly stepped into the breach. Ali won the fight without difficulty but it was now clear that a tougher fight awaited him beyond the ropes. Ali was fast developing into a pariah. Patriotic American organisations actually forced some closed-circuit outlets to boycott the Chuvalo bout. Ali would have to look overseas. Europe was the obvious location and three contests were scheduled within a period of three and a half months. The first was a foregone conclusion: a rematch with Henry Cooper, currently ranked eight in the world. The date: 21 May; the place: Highbury Stadium, home of Arsenal FC.

In actual fact this trip would constitute Ali's third visit to Britain as he

Cooper signs on the dotted line watched by Messrs (from the right) Levene, Wicks and Ali – or at least a life-sized cut-out of the world champion! (Sport & General)

had boxed a number of exhibitions in August 1965. His arrival, on Monday, 9 May, unveiled a vastly different character from that to which his fans had grown accustomed. An uncomfortable flight from Miami could, it's true, be held partly responsible: Ali hated flying and an enforced stopover at Shannon prolonged the journey by over four hours. Yet the soberly dressed young man who walked in to bandy words with the press corps seemed only distantly related to the swaggering jester of 1963: 'Here's Cass – but no gas', reported the *Mirror* with barely concealed astonishment. 'This isn't a new image,' the champ explained. 'The days for hollering are over now that I am no longer campaigning for the title. I've been driven out of my country because of my religious beliefs yet every other country in the world welcomes me. It's a strange feeling. All I ask is the same treatment and respect in my country that other boxers and athletes get from Uncle Sam. My religion is against war and I am within my legal rights to claim exemption on the basis of being a conscientious objector. If I weren't the heavyweight champion of the world there would be none of this fuss. While I'm here in Britain I don't want to be bothered with questions about my personal affairs, such as the draft case and my divorce. I'm here to defend my title and that old man Henry Cooper had better watch out. I'm feeling real mean.' What chance did Cooper have of landing the 'Ammer to conclusive effect this time up? 'Anyone who dares step into the ring with me must have a chance. But I won't be caught again. This time I'm the champ. Then I was only a contender. I plan to be fast and on my guard all the time. I am light and hard and ready to rumble.' Then questions broached stonier ground. Why have you changed your name? 'Cassius only meant dirt with no ingredients. "Muhammad" means one worthy of praise; "Ali" was the name of a great general.' Why did you become a Black Muslim? 'I am not a Black Muslim: I am a Muslim. I am not here to answer questions on religion. You should be ashamed of yourself.' Do you regard this fight as between a black boxer and a white boxer? 'You look too intelligent to ask a dumb question like that.' Thankfully, an air of levity and a trace of the old banter surfaced when someone enquired about the troublesome flight. 'I was asked to say a prayer or recite a verse from the bible. I answered that I can only do one thing religious and that is take up the collection.'

Having fled one 'political' hornets' nest back home Ali discovered he had stumbled across another, albeit less threatening, in Britain. A row over television coverage had met stalemate and government assistance was being sought to break the deadlock. Harry Levene was promoting the fight in association with Jarvis Astaire's Viewsport company, which held exclusive rights to show the bout live with commentary from Reg Gutteridge. His audience was expected to include 30,000 subscribers to Pay TV in and around London plus a further 40,000 spread among 17 Rank cinemas throughout the country (Birmingham, Manchester, Leeds, Leicester, Nottingham, Southampton, Cardiff, Newcastle, Glasgow, Coventry, Norwich and London) where tickets ranged from two guineas to five guineas; 20 million Americans were expected to view the fight via the Early Bird satellite. Astaire offered the fight for network transmission at any hour after one p.m. the following day; the asking price was £32,000. The offer was rejected out of hand by both the BBC and ITV. They protested to the Postmaster General – Anthony Wedgwood Benn. A two-hour meeting failed to achieve a compromise, however, and Britain's first heavyweight title fight since 1908 was lost to television viewers. Angelo Dundee expressed disbelief: 'It doesn't make sense to me. The champ has a lot of fans in Europe and I can't see why they shouldn't see him. After all, this is the greatest heavyweight fight you've ever had in Europe. As far as I'm concerned it means we are losing a lot of money but for the champion it's a matter of pride.'

Ali himself seemed oblivious to the shenanigans and headed for the Piccadilly Hotel to be met by 500-odd fans who succeeded in blocking the entrance and trapping him in his limo. Once safely inside, Ali retired for some badly needed sleep; outside his room a two-feet-high Irish leprechaun stood guard, bought for £3 during that Shannon stopover!

The next 11 days comprised the routine treadmill of roadwork, sparring, interviews and showboating. Along with Jimmy Ellis (and occasionally Jim Brown, one time NFL star running back with the Cleveland Browns, in England in his new guise as an actor to shoot the all-action picture, *The Dirty Dozen*), Ali would complete 105 miles around Hyde Park. In the gym – motivated by a photo of the 'Ammer's 1963 'andiwork pinned to the wall – he pounded away on his own heavy bag, that had been especially brought over for him, in between 73 rounds of sparring. 'I've never seen a guy roll his head away from punches like that,' observed one visitor, former middleweight champion of the world, Terry Downes. 'Fantastic!' Another admiring onlooker was 72-year-old Georges Carpentier, once heavyweight champion of Europe and light-heavyweight champion of the world: 'What can I say to such a great fighter? You are the first man of your weight I have seen who could win a fight with his legs.'

Jimmy Ellis was Ali's regular sparring partner – except for one memorable occasion. A young unbeaten light-heavy from Canning Town was allowed to share the ring and he promptly incited gasps of amazement by putting Ali on the deck. The young pugilist was Jimmy Tibbs, destined to make his name as a trainer of champions rather than to become one himself. 'I wish it had been for real! It was all tongue-in-cheek. I was an up-and-coming fighter of 19 or 20 and was appearing on the same bill. Mickey Duff arranged the sparring. Ali was far bigger than me, naturally, but I'd spar with anyone and it was good publicity – for both myself and Ali. Him going down was not set up as far as I know but I didn't hit him with an actual real punch. It shocked me as much as everyone else: he went down spectacularly! It was a publicity stunt. It was a great honour to be in the same ring for a couple of rounds, even if it was just for fun. We shook hands but have never met since, though I was in Frank Bruno's corner for the Witherspoon fight when Ali was at ringside.'

As usual, Ali's White City HQ became the hottest ticket in town: 'The court of Super-MACC' (Muhammad Ali Cassius Clay), as Peter Wilson dubbed it. Besides the familiar faces were reporters from as far afield as Russia, Pakistan and Australia. 'It's not easy to meet the President of Egypt, the Queen of England or the President of the United States. But it has to be harder to meet the heavyweight champion of the WORLD!' Told by the Russian journalist that Soviet boxers were studying films of him in order to improve their technique Ali warned: 'But it's not just a question of copying. The way I box I make it look easy. But the fella must be in condition. You gotta do your roadwork. Then you can hit and move and not be hit. Too many of the old heavyweights moved flat-footed and that's why they got cut eyes, flat noses and cauliflower ears. No natural zip! I'm good for another six years and another three million dollars! The way science is moving mebbe I'll even end up fighting on Mars.'

Once the gloves were laid aside Ali made the customary rounds to satisfy photo opportunities. He paid a visit to the London Free School in Notting Hill; lunched at the House of Commons with Prime Minister Harold Wilson; attended a reception at the Café Royal, where Harry Carpenter, chairman of the British Boxing Writers' Club, presented him with a trophy and a club tie; and dropped in at Lord's for a Test match between England and the West Indies. 'I like cricket. I reckon our baseball must have been based on this game. Too slow? I don't think so. Running up as fast as Wes Hall would be good training for me!' However, following two cups of tea and a glass of iced water not even the sight of M.J.K. Smith completing a century could prevent Ali from falling asleep! More to his liking were those evenings free of engagements, as Nick Reekie, the teenage son of Ali's cornerman, fondly recalls: 'I was on school holidays at the time and was allowed to tag along, although I always had to hold Muhammad's hand whenever we crossed a road! Each night we would all eat at Isow's restaurant before usually trooping off to the cinema. Muhammad's favourite was *The Blue Max*, about a First World War flying ace, which he called The Blue "Mac". Dad had worked with Angelo from 1954 as his agent over here; he also worked as a security clerk at one of Terry Downes's betting shops, where Jimmy Tibbs was the board-boy. Being in Muhammad's camp didn't go down too well with everyone, though, and a few words were passed to that effect by Danny Holland, Cooper's trainer.'

For a Londoner to side with the opposition against one of his own was

The Reekie family has a visitor: (left to right) Dick, Ali; daughter, Jane, and her husband,
Mick, and son, Nick (Nick Reekie Collection)

Nick Reekie eyes the camera rather than Ali's blurring hand-speed (Nick Reekie Collection)

deemed a mortal sin by some. 'A Cockney against Cooper' was how Reg Gutteridge's piece in the *Evening News* described the tiff. However, belying a pint-sized frame and professorial demeanour (he was a columnist for *Boxing Illustrated* and *Boxing News*) nothing was likely to frighten the 48-year-old, Limehouse-born Reekie. During the war he had served as a radio operator and air-gunner in Abyssinia, Syria and North Africa; and in 1964 he even plucked up the courage to second Willie Pastrano in a world title fight against his own boss, Terry Downes. Said Dundee: 'Dick is my buddy, a good omen. I like him in my corner for company.'

The Cockney in Cooper's corner, the 'Bishop of Bash' Jim Wicks, was not short of a word or three! 'Cooper will knock him out. He is a changed man. I have never seen a boxer so confident. These days he just walks out from his corner and knocks them over, and he will do the same with Clay.' Even 'Enery himself exuded the air of a man who believed his moment of glory was at hand. 'No, I don't think much about losing. I knocked him down and that must worry him a bit even though he's champion now. He's very fast and I may have to chase him. But if I catch him I think he'll go. All I ask of the referee is that he doesn't stop it if Clay cuts me, no matter how bad it looks. I want this decision left to my corner.' The official in the hot seat would be 54-year-old George Smith of Edinburgh, a referee for 15 years but of 'star' rating only since December 1964; he had controlled just two

championship bouts (one bantam and one middle) and had called a premature halt to both. Ali demanded a 20-foot ring – as big as a ballroom, said Cooper – which Levene was obliged to have custom-made for £500; he wanted plenty of space in which to elude the 'Ammer. Nevertheless, a cartoon he hastily drew for his artist friend Leroy Nieman suggested otherwise. It depicted him imploring of a Cooper exiting through the ropes in a daze: 'Come back, Henery. Don't run.' Ali took 15 minutes to knock up the drawing in the lounge of his hotel. Said Nieman: 'How can you value something like this? You might as well try to put a price on the champion's right hand. It's this sort of touch that shows the champ's sense of humour.' The *Daily Mirror* carried a copy in its fight-day issue. Cooper, too, was receiving plenty of media attention: he was that day's 'castaway' on BBC radio's *Desert Island Discs* and he also guested on a pre-recorded edition of BBC's hit television comedy show *Not Only, But Also* with Peter Cook and Dudley Moore.

A crowd estimated at around 42,000 packed into Highbury to witness only the ninth British challenge for the Greatest Prize in Sport since it was initially contested under the Marquess of Queensberry rules in 1892 – and the first in this country since Tommy Burns knocked out Jack Palmer in the fourth round of their London contest on 10 February 1908. Brian London's 11th-round knockout at the hands of Floyd Patterson was the most recent

World's Largest Evening Sale

The Evening News
and STAR

LONDON SATURDAY MAY 21 1966

PRICE 4d.

stainless steel
CASHMORES

Henry and Cassius meet again after three years

Clay has been world champion since 1964

Cooper has been the home ace since 1960

Cooper has won 38 of his 45 bouts

Clay has won all his 23 paid fights

In 1954 Cassius changed his name to Muhammad Ali

How 34, Clay won an Olympic Gold at 16

FIGHT OF THE CENTURY

CLAY MEETS COOPER AT HIGHBURY

HOW THEY COMPARE

MUHAMMAD ALI		HENRY COOPER
24 (Jan 17, 1942)	AGE	32 (May 3, 1934)
14st. 8lb.	WEIGHT (approx)	13st. 6lb.
6ft. 3in.	HEIGHT	6ft. 1½in.
79in.	REACH	73in.
42½in.	CHEST (normal)	42in.
44in.	CHEST (expanded)	44in.
17½in.	NECK	17½in.
34in.	WAIST	34in.
15in.	BICEPS	15in.
9in.	WRIST	8in.
17in.	CALF	16in.
12½in.	FOREARM	12in.
9½in.	ANKLE	10in.

The World Champion

Henry's left hook in action at Wembley

The British Challenger

ARSENAL STADIUM № 1161
HIGHBURY, N.5

HARRY LEVENE
presents
Heavyweight Championship of the World
MUHAMMAD ALI (formerly
(U.S.A.) Champion v. Cassius Clay)
HENRY COOPER (Gt. Britain)
15 — 3-minute Rounds Challenger
SATURDAY, MAY 21st, 1966
Gates Open 6 p.m.   Commences 8 p.m.
It is in your interest to be at the Stadium early.
GILLESPIE ROAD GROUND
Admission £2-2-0 (STANDING) TURNSTILE S
Issued subject to conditions on reverse.
THIS PORTION TO BE RETAINED
This Ticket must be intact when presented at the Turnstile.

(Perry Aghajanoff Collection)

Second time round, Ali is much cagier (Mirror Syndication International)

(Indianapolis, 1 May 1959); before that were Don Cockell, stopped by Rocky Marciano in nine (San Francisco, 16 May 1955); Tommy Farr, a loser on points to Joe Louis (New York, 30 August 1937); Palmer; Gunner James Moir, like Palmer, kayoed by Burns (London, 2 December 1907); Bob Fitzsimmons, who was knocked out in the eighth when attempting to regain the title from James J. Jeffries (San Francisco, 25 July 1902); and Charlie Mitchell, knocked out by James J. Corbett in the third (Jacksonville, 25 January 1894). The Cornish-born Fitzsimmons, of course, had previously won the championship from Corbett on 17 March 1897, having been obliged to take out American citizenship in order to get his chance.

In keeping with this rare privilege of a world heavyweight championship bout on British soil fight fans were paying between two and 20 guineas a ticket, amounting to a gate of £252,000; with various worldwide transmissions added on, Levene and Astaire expected to gross £400,000. Ali's purse was a reputed £215,000, Cooper's £40,000. 'Ali was a magnificent PR man for the promotion,' recalls Astaire. 'I had first met him, briefly, in 1963 when he fought Cooper the first time. I was not involved in that promotion but, of course, I saw a lot of him in 1966. He was so professional and dedicated to making the promotion a success. He was on a percentage but in talking-up the fight he was not just calculating how much money it would bring. He really wanted people to come and see him beat Cooper. He meant every word of what he said and despite the knockdown in 1963 he had no fear of losing to Cooper. Today, boxers just say those sort of things for effect. He didn't. After we sent him his money his lawyers wrote back saying it was the first time his pay had exceeded the guarantee. From then on everyone wanted to get in on the act but Ali's management always made sure I got the rights to show his fights. Even so I refused the Berbick fight because it shouldn't have happened and though I took the Holmes fight I very much regret having done so to this day.'

What chances had Cooper realistically got? *Boxing News* summarised them as 'a hope, a prayer and a left hook'. According to the bookies they were no better than 6/1; Ali was 10/1 on. The weigh-in, at the Odeon, Leicester Square, for what the *Evening News* billed as the 'Fight of the Century', saw the champion scale 14st 5½lbs to the challenger's 13st 6lbs – eight pounds closer in the weights than for their previous encounter. Cooper was in an ebullient mood. Noticing one solitary black hair on Ali's chest he leaned forward and gave it a tweak: 'Oh, look, he's a man all right. He's got a hair on his chest!'

Ali was not amused.

'My lords, ladies and gentlemen . . .' Those traditional, spine-tingling words from MC Charles Freen rang out across the airwaves signalling to all us less privileged fight fans that the action was about to commence at long last. Such was the throng that Cooper's entrance had been delayed ten minutes while a path to the ring was cleared. Preceded by the Union Jack, he ducks between the ropes to reveal a crossed pair of the same flags on the back of his robe: Ali arrives in a simple white outfit. The preliminaries, thankfully, are kept to a minimum. Just a few celebrities: Rocky Marciano, Georges Carpentier, Ingemar Johansson, Karl Mildenberger, Billy Walker. The national anthems are played and it's time for touching gloves.

The pattern of the fight is instantly established and surprises no one. Cooper stalks, Ali retreats. 'Enery throws a punch, Muhammad arches his back and leans away, out of reach. The hunter has two options. Either he must lunge with his right lead in order to make contact or he must rush his prey and risk the consequences. Ali has absorbed the lessons of 18 June 1963. At the first inkling of close-quarter danger he holds Cooper in a vice until ordered to break, and then he steps well back as if his life depended upon it. Every blow landed by Cooper triggers a volcanic outburst of cheering but although he gets through with single shots he just cannot double-up. Ali is too quick; too slippery. He is up on his toes dancing to a non-stop beat we cannot hear but is self-evident from the bouncing rhythm of his floppy white bootlaces. From the waist up Ali resembles a cobra, a sleek, brown King Cobra, constantly swaying this way and that before occasionally striking to venomous effect. Toward the end of the round a clubbing overarm right, brought down and across the angle of Cooper's left eyebrow, serves as a warning.

Rounds two to five pass strictly according to the plot – which suddenly thickens 45 seconds into the sixth. Ali follows up a left lead with another of those slashing right hands, which hones in on Cooper's fragile left eyebrow. Cooper hustles Ali into a corner like a man possessed; it appears their heads may have come into contact; but, whatever the case, on returning to the centre of the ring Cooper is seen to be shaking his head. He recognises that old, familiar sensation; the worst feeling he knows in boxing. His eye is gushing blood like a burst pipe. 'Ripped open like a zip-fastener,' was how Reg Gutteridge evocatively described it. 'Man, I could hear him bleeding,' was the champion's equally vivid description. George Smith takes a look and, somewhat astonishingly, waves Cooper on. Ali now starts to come forward and the fight surely cannot last much longer: one minute 38 seconds of the sixth round marks the official end – 'with the suddenness of an avalanche' in Hugh McIlvanney's phrase – of Cooper's quest. Afterwards the vanquished greets the victor in his dressing-room with the words: 'It was a pity. We was really enjoying ourselves. But I'd have done the same to you if I could.' The next morning Cooper attended Guy's Hospital where four deep stitches and a dozen on the surface were required to close the gash. Ali was adamant: 'I told the referee he should stop it. He looked at him but let him go on. He was wrong. I ran, only defending myself, hoping the ref would stop it. It is against my religion to

Cooper's left eye is 'ripped open like a zip-fastener' (Popperfoto)

attack a man who is bleeding like that. I had to throw a few punches but I did not aim for the cut because I knew the fight was over. Henry hurt me just once. It was a left hook in the third. But I was too fast for him tonight. He couldn't catch me again. I opened the cut with a left-right combination. I wanted the referee to stop it straightaway. The blood disturbed me a lot. It was pure violence and that was against my personal feelings and my religion. Henry's a good fighter but his flesh is weak. If the fight had not been stopped I am confident I would have knocked him out in the ninth or tenth round. The first thing I had to do afterwards was wash my hair. It was full of blood – his blood.' Ali's white trunks were likewise caked in blood. They eventually came into the possession of John Lennon who auctioned them to raise money to fight for world peace; he was, he said, glad to see Cooper's blood put to a good cause.

The press looked kindly on Cooper's plucky effort. *Boxing News* spoke for most via its front page sentiment, 'Hard Luck, Henry'; even the *New York Daily News* paid tribute to England's 'gallant, fearless greengrocer'. And Ali's opinion? 'Tough, tough fighter. If he didn't cut so easily he might have been a leading contender.' That assessment finds no disfavour with Henry Cooper. 'Ali didn't know too much for me. It was a physical thing that let me down, having prominent bones and weak skin tissue around the eyes. He respected me in the '66 fight, he was much more subdued than in '63, and was obviously well schooled for the return. He had been very "novicey" in the first fight but in the second he held me like a vice till the ref shouted break. The only time he came forward really slinging punches was when the eye was pumping blood. It was the heel of his glove, chopping down, that caused it. I was slinging a left hook and he went to knock it away with a right hand and that's how it happened. He was the fastest-moving heavyweight in history. He had the speed of a middleweight. There's been no one else like him.'

Any suspicion that the cut may have resulted from a clash of heads instead of a fist was soon dispelled by slow-motion replays. Ali himself scrutinised the footage in the company of Peter Wilson. 'You can all see it was a punch and not my head that caused the injury. You can see how my body had slid across Cooper's and my head is in no way in any contact with Cooper's head.' All those who attended one of 200 Rank cinemas in the next few days were able to verify the fact: film of the fight was added to the programme as a 'special presentation'. In its own right the film made a profit of £93,000. As Henry Cooper said: 'Everyone earns when they fight Ali.'

A PUBLIC EXECUTION

At the age of 32 Brian London could no longer accurately be described as the *enfant terrible* of British boxing but he still came pretty close. Our Brian did not quite comply with the establishment's idea of the noble art's acceptable public face. A bluff Lancashire lad from Blackpool, with scant regard for airs and graces, here was a man who preferred his home comforts and engagements at the Liverpool Stadium or the King's Hall, Manchester, to the capital's high profile venues.

London and controversy were not strangers to one another. As an amateur – fighting under his real name of Harper – he had won the 1954 Empire Games title but his rough-house tactics once caused a riot in an international against Italy at the National Theatre, Milan. According to Harry Gibbs, the British team's trainer, London hit Nino Bozzano while he was still on his stool; butted him; and then thumbed him in the eye! The carabinieri were enlisted to get London out of the building. The infamous, undignified brawl between both fighters and their respective cornermen after London was stopped by Dick Richardson in a 1960 European title bout also provided boxing with the kind of tainted image the BBBC was desperately trying to eliminate. Only the previous year London had cocked another snoot at the Board by going through with an unsanctioned challenge for Floyd Patterson's world crown. The American press gave London a hammering: 'Before he and Patterson met we didn't know how London could fight and afterwards we still don't know!' Patterson, also, gave London a hammering, knocking him out in 57 seconds of round 11: 'He had never thrown a really damaging punch.' Finally, the BBBC gave London a hammering: it fined him £1,000.

Now, seven years on, he was preparing to mount a second challenge for 'The Greatest Prize in Sport'. Although the BBBC sanctioned this challenge almost everyone else to a man shook their heads and sharply sucked in air. Yes, London's world ranking of nine was only one place below Cooper's but 'Enery was the British champion and did possess the 'Ammer. What had London to offer? British and Empire champion for six months after stopping Joe Erskine in June 1958, he lost the titles to Cooper on points and met the same fate when attempting to regain them in February 1964. London's career record stood at 35 wins (14 by knockout) from 48 contests; Patterson was the single opponent who had him counted out. On his most recent appearance, on 21 June in Liverpool, his American opponent Amos Johnson was disqualified in the seventh. London had, in fact, been in with quite a few Americans. Besides Patterson and Johnson he had fought other top-notchers like Eddie Machen (lost in five), Thad Spencer (outpointed) and Willie Pastrano (won and lost); he had kayoed Roger Rischer and Pete Rademacher and secured points victories over Tom McNeeley, Don Warner and Howard King. This last one came on a rain-sodden outdoor bill at Blackpool with both boxers scorning boots and the referee protected by a mackintosh! On the credit side, that defeat by Spencer (ranked five in the world) was London's only defeat in the last two years.

Nevertheless, to all but London's nearest and dearest the bout bore all the hallmarks of a mismatch. *The Times* made no bones about it: 'At 32 he seems to be coming to the end of a turbulent and sometimes controversial career in the ring whereas his undefeated opponent retains the ability and undaunted spirit of an eager young thoroughbred.' Peter Wilson mused: 'How is London going to slow down a giant streak of black lightning? How can you grasp a handful of quicksilver or encompass a puff of smoke drifting in the breeze?' But, of course, Ali was desperate for fights beyond the reach of American authorities. Twenty-eight years after the event Brian London recalls: 'Although I had only seen Ali on television I knew I'd not got the ability to beat him. But I was a strong fighter and I always thought I'd go the distance. And I think Ali's camp thought I could be trouble. Angelo Dundee also trained Pastrano and knew what I could do. I should have learned from the Patterson fight, though, and I didn't. I needed someone to look after me. I went to the States for the Patterson fight without sparring partners and they gave me a 15-stone gorilla – and I was fighting a fast man of 13 stone! I should have trained differently. And I made the same mistake preparing for Ali. I stayed in Blackpool and didn't get the right people around me. I needed a Duff or a Lawless.'

Formal announcement of the fight came on 29 June with Jack Solomons mentioning Blackpool and Manchester as possible venues, but within 24 hours the 18,474-seater Earls Court was confirmed for 6 August; London would receive £40,000. Tickets ranged from two to 20 guineas and 20 cinemas (belonging to the Granada group) would cater for an additional 50,000 customers; France, Italy, Sweden, Switzerland and Germany would also show the contest live in addition to the USA.

Ali arrived on 25 July to a 'Welcome to Britain' breakfast in the revolving restaurant 35 floors up at the top of the recently opened 620-feet Post Office Tower. After devouring four fruit juices, kidneys, eggs, bacon and kippers he turned his attentions to London. 'I wish I could see Blackpool and Brian London from here. I had hoped to size him up; it put me off my plans that he did not turn up for breakfast. I'm taking him real serious. He is big and strong and can take a punch and I expect the fight to go longer than the

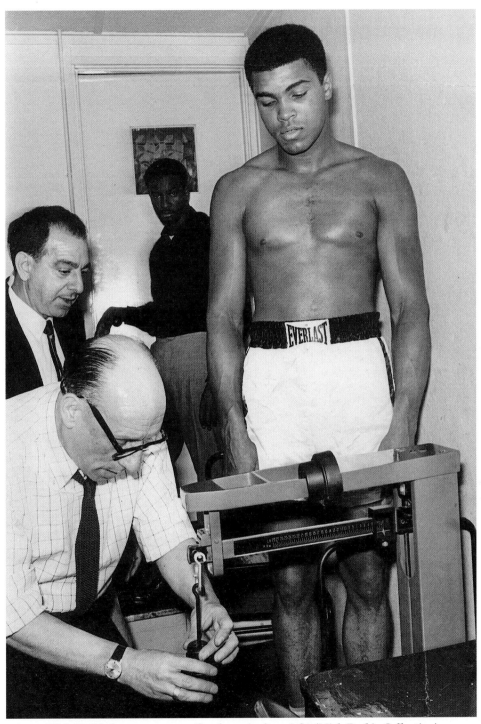

Dick Reekie keeps an eye on the champion's weight (Nick Reekie Collection)

*There are always
fans to meet
(Paddy Monaghan
Collection)*

ones with Cooper. It could go ten rounds or it could even go the distance because I am not a heavy puncher. I dance a lot and flip a lot. I'm fast and classy! But I must beware. This is the time that champions slip. I must be on my guard. We can expect a good little scuffle. London's a tough fellow. I understand he does not cut and is not easy put down. I would have liked the chance of staring London down today but I guess that will have to wait. If London beats me that's it!'

London sent a letter of apology. Needless to say, he was at home in Blackpool. 'I have no desire to see Clay before the weigh-in, when I hope he behaves himself. He has won most of his fights by frightening people with his big mouth. He's called me too small, too fat and too ugly. I don't want to get mad with him and upset myself by meeting him before the fight. I've been told I should retire at least eight times; but as long as Clay doesn't hurt me too much I'll carry on collecting the cash. I'm after the money like the rest. Anybody who says he likes boxing needs his brains tested. I've backed myself to win £10,000. I've never seen Clay take a good punch really well. I know he can't punch and words won't hurt me. He can't insult me. I'm too ignorant.'

You did not have to be a clairvoyant to realise that every last syllable of Jack Solomons's legendary sales patter would be necessary to drum up interest in this particular fight. Surely, London hadn't a prayer. The *Daily Mirror*'s somewhat facetious angle was to enquire of its readers: 'How would *you* send the British Bulldog in to win? Entries on a postcard, please, no more than 50 words. Twenty winners will each receive a 20 guineas ringside seat.' The *Mirror* promptly received an entry from one individual certainly not in need of a seat: Muhammad Ali.

> *How would you send London out to win?*
> *By keeping cool and not getting hit on the chin.*
> *It will be an exciting night on August 6 in the huge Earls Court;*
> *On that night the world will see us as the biggest sport.*
> *Brian! You said you feel confident because England is your homeland,*
> *But I have an equaliser . . . it's my fast left hand.*
> *Why are you talking about knocking me out and all that jive?*
> *Man, if you dreamed you did you better apologise!*
> *Liston, Patterson, Chuvalo, Cooper didn't have a chance*
> *Because it's impossible to lick me if you can't dance.*
> *I used to pop off, show off, holler and brag;*
> *Now you're talking and it is your jaw I'm out to tag!*
> *When we meet forget your people and hop around like an Easter bunny,*
> *In order to save some of that hard-earned and saved-up money!*

Ali's inevitable loquacity warranted instant disqualification for

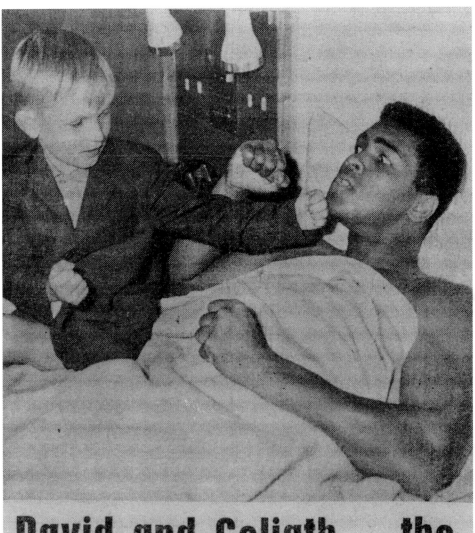

David and Goliath...the big fight 24 hours early

*Six-year-old David Walker tags his man; 11 years later so would his dad, Johnny
(Johnny Walker Collection)*

exceeding 50 words. London's reply – at 38 words – fell comfortably within the limit.

Two guns and a club I don't need but your feet and your speed you will need,
To move out of the way of two fists made for Clay
And two feet that will dance on this day.

At least with the World Cup final between England and West Germany now a thing of the past press coverage began to pick up. However, even the mellifluous words of Peter Wilson could do little to camouflage the distinctly low-key atmosphere which had enveloped the fight and threatened to destroy any remaining credibility. Wilson journeyed north to Pontin's Holiday Camp in Blackpool where London's training was being conducted in a glass-walled sun lounge known as the Sunset Café. True to form, London failed to train on the day of Wilson's visit; he had strained a back muscle. The fight was now just four days away. 'I used to be sullen when I was surrounded by press asking questions. I was young then. I used to get mad when you wrote that I had a spare tyre round my middle. I'm not fooling myself. I know Clay's the favourite. But don't forget he was the 7/1 underdog when he fought Sonny Liston the first time. Outsiders do win. How am I going to fight? I've got to go out and take it to him. I don't think I can outpoint him unless he's taken me for a complete mug. I'll be trying to press him all the time. He doesn't seem to be a great puncher and I haven't often been badly hurt. I'm as strong as Clay, that I am. He's got a longer reach, though.' Wilson left Pontin's believing London was a more mature boxer than of old: 'I don't think he'll freeze up on the night.' London departed on Friday – by train not by helicopter as he had hoped – after a civic reception at which the mayor had presented him with a lucky glass horseshoe.

Ali, meanwhile, had put on a show of skipping and shadow-boxing when Henry Cooper came a-calling; before receiving a bloodied mouth from Jimmy Ellis during sparring. The man they couldn't 'gag' saw little to enthuse about when he, too, attended Ali's court, although the substitution of sublime artist for a plodding artisan did inspire Wilson to the kind of evocative simile with which his name had become synonymous: 'Somehow a little of the original sparkle, which used to surround the young Clay like the bubbles bursting round the rim of a glass of champagne, has gone rather flat.' Ali admitted that the initial rush of excitement which had accompanied the title was, indeed, beginning to wear thin. 'I was excited when I won the title, and in my first few defences. But, now, it's the challengers who get the fun trying to beat me. I am not in top shape for London. But I wasn't in top shape for Cooper; but, then, I have never been in absolutely top condition. I could always work a little harder, do an extra couple of rounds, be trimmer and faster. If he fights dirty I'll fight dirty. We'll both fight dirty! I tell him to put his wife and children at ringside and to remember that he is fighting for them; if you hit the champion right and he doesn't fall – run! I am not immortal but I know that whatever London has to fight for I have ten times more at stake.'

Duty done, Ali dropped in on the Hertfordshire set of *The Dirty Dozen* for a chat with occasional running-mate Jim Brown and his screen co-star Clint Walker. As far as the small screen was concerned ATV had launched a company to be called World Wide Sports in order to purchase exclusive rights to the contest, which would be shown 24 hours later on the ITV network.

The man given the honour of officiating in the ring was 45-year-old Harry Gibbs, whose no-nonsense manner was what one would expect from a Bermondsey-born dock worker. It was Gibbs, in his capacity as team trainer, who had shepherded London out of that Milan arena. He had been refereeing since 1957 and took charge of his first world title fight after a mere seven years' experience; this would be his second of 1966, having controlled the McGowan-Burunni encounter six months earlier. He had never shared a ring with Ali but he had officiated on the undercard of both Cooper fights, which afforded plenty of opportunity to observe the champion at close quarters upon completing his own job. 'It had always been my ambition to referee a world heavyweight title fight. But up until 1966 I did not think I had a chance the way our heavyweights were fighting. Before the fight I visited the dressing-rooms with the Board's chief inspector and Ali says to me: "Now look, Mr Ref, I hear this guy hits to the kidney and butts." He always was a brash, cheeky customer! So, I gave him one of my coldest stares and said: "Right, Sonny. You do your job and I'll do mine." Though to be honest I think I put it a trifle stronger than that! Poor old Brian was not given much time to bend or twist the rules, let alone break them.'

Apart from counting to ten over the prostrate figure of London early in the third round the only energy Gibbs expended was in walking around the ring. Only once was he obliged to come between the fighters – when London clumsily wrapped himself round Ali's back during the second. Ali had entered the ring with an advantage of 9½lb in weight (at 14 stone 13½lb he was 8lb heavier than for Cooper), seven inches in reach and goodness knows how much in speed of thought, hands and feet. Once again he had demanded a larger than normal ring in which to best capitalise upon them.

An estimated 13 million people tuned their radios to the Light Programme but only about 9,000 actually filed into Earls Court. The half-empty arena possessed a suitably haunted air as London materialised in a white hooded robe decorated with a bulldog's head. Those at ringside

At the weigh-in Brian London looks confident, Jack Solomons looks happy (Popperfoto)

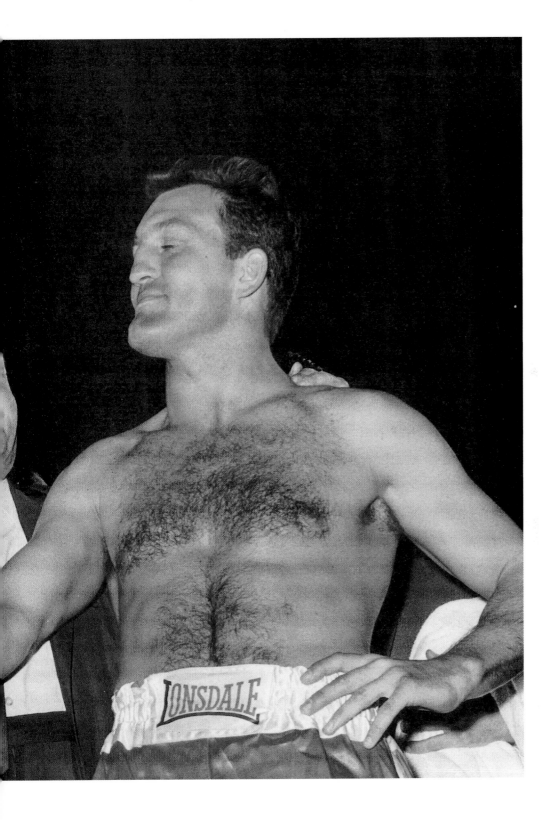

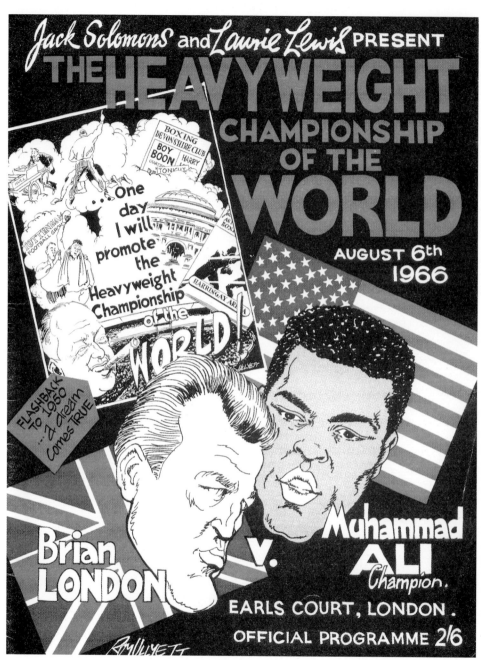

(Perry Aghajanoff Collection)

Angelo Dundee, Ali and Dick Reekie 'raring to go'? (Nick Reekie Collection)

averred that the logo was the most aggressive thing associated with Brian London on the night of 6 August 1966.

London was counted out after one minute 40 seconds of the third round, having landed, said some observers, only four meaningful punches. *The Times* rewarded the contest with a paltry four column inches, which included the damning judgment: 'A public execution is an unwholesome spectacle and the defeat of Brian London amounted to little more. Aficionados of the bullring would have appreciated the decisiveness and swiftness of the moment of truth. But even the best of matadors need a brave bull to demonstrate their full skills.' The *Daily Telegraph*'s Donald Saunders declared: 'This was a perfect example of how to be a good British loser. For most of this humiliatingly one-sided affair London presented Clay with what must be the slowest moving, easiest-to-hit target the champion has been lucky enough to encounter since leaving the amateur ranks. Thirty-five minutes after heaving himself off his stool at the start of the fight, London was paying handsome tribute to the champion in Cassius Clay's dressing-room. London, already dressed in a checked suit, told Clay: "You are a great champion. I would like a return fight. Now I must get off home because I have got three children to think of." It was all admirably sporting. Alas, it did not compensate for what had happened earlier. Had London's performance inside the ring been as efficient as it was in Clay's dressing-room one might not feel so sorry for the reputation of British heavyweight boxing.' The *Mirror*'s headline referred to a 'Black eye for British boxing' beneath which Wilson wrote: 'Clay exposed him as a lumbering, bumbling, unskilled workman – a boxer who couldn't box. His competitiveness seems to ooze out of him when he has a back-to-the-wall, do-or-die engagement on his hands.' *Boxing News* summarised the event even more cruelly: 'London pathetic.' With precious little genuine action to describe, Wilson exercised his right of poetic licence. 'Have you ever seen a lamb trying to bite a dog?/Clay dances off the ropes like Blondin/a right hand landed as though London's jaw was a magnet and Clay's gloves were powdered with iron filings.'

When the champion suddenly trapped London in his own corner within 30 seconds of the start of the third and decided to beat out a 14-punch tattoo on the unfortunate Briton's head it did not seem a moment too soon. Even so, Gibbs later expressed surprise at its finality: 'I must say it did not look as if he had been hurt all that badly but who are we to know how hard Ali could hit? So far as London is concerned I believe it is unfair to him to say that his heart was not in it. I feel the problem may well have been stage fright: he had been psyched by Ali.' Ali's own analysis likewise damned London with faint praise: 'Seems I'm fighting here every month. As to the suggestion that I haven't trained properly, well, just see what happened tonight! I weighed more than usual so I could punch harder but the final

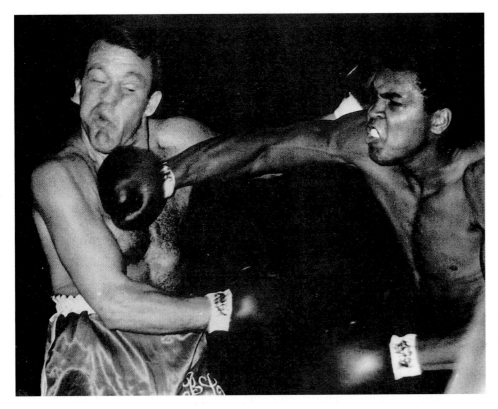

The 'public execution' is about to be concluded (Perry Aghajanoff Collection)

punches weren't hard ones; just snappy ones – very fast! I prepared to take him in round six.' And London? His immediate reaction – due in the main to that extraordinarily hasty exit from the stadium – cut no ice whatsoever with the press: 'Clay was colossal. I've fought the best heavyweights from all over the world but he's colossal. I knew he was fast but not that fast! He threw so many punches I didn't know where they were coming from. I did my best but tonight I fought the greatest fighter in the world. He hits you so often you're dizzy! It wasn't the hardness of the punches, it was the flurry of them. Meet him again? Sure, as long as he ties a 50lb weight to each leg! He hit me with two great punches harder than I've had to take before and I did not know where I was. They never gave me a chance of winning and I didn't win, so no one is disappointed. The BBBC sanctioned the fight. It was up to them not me. It's not my fault if it was a mismatch.'

On arrival at Blackpool station only one fan was there to greet him; 14-year-old Christine Smith clutching her autograph book. In it London wrote: 'Be Friendly'. If only the press had been so friendly.

The years have done nothing to dim Brian London's sense of shame. 'It was the worst night of my boxing career. I can never forgive myself. I fought the world's best and was never bothered with any of them but this was a disaster. I was devastated to get beat like I did. I disgraced myself.

77

He overawed me. The whole top and bottom of it was I was just not good enough. He was too fast. If he had done the same as he did against Cooper and Mildenberger – stood off and taken the piss for a few rounds – I might have done better but he didn't. He came out and had a go at me, and for a man of 15 stone to come at you like a bloody welterweight was something special. If I'd stood there for 15 rounds and got sliced to bits they'd have all been saying what a great guy I was. But I didn't and they crucified me for it.'

There can be no doubt who 'they' were: the boxing establishment and the boxing media which is firmly entrenched in the south – south of Blackpool at any rate. As far as the fight itself is concerned London does have a point: he did come forward and he did try to reach Ali. It was not a case of him standing there like a coconut in a coconut shy. Ali came out dancing and throwing leather: not only stinging jabs but also numerous right hands, ripping and clubbing punches of a ferocity he had not shown in the Cooper fight. Ali was in his prime. You could have attached London to a ring post with a rubber band and twanged him round the ring and still Ali would have nailed him.

Whatever condition it was in that night at Earls Court London's heart summoned up the wherewithal to fight on. Nine subsequent visits to the ring, however, yielded just two victories and as the '60s drew to a close a string of inside-the-distance defeats culminated in a fifth-round stoppage against a young St Ives prospect 15 years his junior called Joe Bugner. London absorbed 17 consecutive blows without reply before the referee – his old chum Harry Gibbs – saved him from further punishment. At the sorry conclusion of his 58th fight, and one month short of his 36th birthday, London walked to the centre of the ring and announced his retirement with the words: 'Thanks for having me.'

THE PEOPLE'S CHAMPION

The BBC's seven-part series of 1968 entitled *The Richest Prize in Sport* was compulsory viewing. Particularly part seven. This chapter was devoted to Muhammad Ali, at the time languishing in exile. The banishment would last over three and a half years. Stripped of his titles on 28 April 1967 for refusing induction into the US Armed Forces, Ali and boxing would see no more of each other until 26 October 1970. 'Surely, you miss boxing?' Harry Carpenter pressed him at the end of the programme. 'No, Harry,' replied Ali. 'Boxing misses me.' For boxing read Britain. As the sport's governing bodies deprived Ali of his titles and livelihood the US Government relieved him of his passport. 'I always knew that God had a purpose for me. I thought it was to be a boxer but now I know it's more – to be a world man. I'm not an ordinary mortal. I am bigger than sport itself. Why did I join the Muslims? When I came back from the Olympics in Rome with a gold medal I couldn't sit down and drink a cup of coffee in a place in our town of Louisville. I don't smoke. I don't drink or go to places where there are prostitutes. There's never been a breath of scandal about me – but there are people who hate me. We don't believe in violence; we don't carry weapons. Bullets can't hurt Muslims. If the prophet Elijah Muhammad told me to stop boxing I'd do it at once.'

Ever since February 1966 when Ali had been goaded by persistent media interrogation into a frank admission – 'I ain't got no quarrel with them Viet Cong. The real enemies of my people are right here, not in Vietnam.' – the establishment's tourniquet had been applied tighter and tighter. His pacifist Islamic principles hardly endeared him to an America losing her sons in an unpopular war. In August 1966, during the lead-up to the Brian London fight, Peter Wilson penned an article spotlighting 'the champion fighting on two fronts', while *Daily Express* cartoonist Roy Ullyatt entertained us with a cigar-chomping US master sergeant informing a dejected Ali: 'Don't feel unloved . . . the Army still wants you.' Ali's stance, though inevitably vilified in the US press, was viewed more liberally by British newspapers. The day after Ali refused to take that one step forward in Houston as his 'name and service' was called *The Times* devoted its editorial to the 'Called-Up Champion'. It ran: 'His manner in and out of the ring has often been infuriating – deliberately so. He has shown himself vain, cruel and continuously provocative. But his manner does not mean that his religion is a pose or his conscience cultivated. It would be just as wrong for Muhammad Ali to be given special treatment because he was a nuisance as it would be to hound him into the Army to teach him a lesson.'

Ali also attracted support from mathematician and philosopher Bertrand Russell, a lifelong pacifist who had himself suffered imprisonment during the First World War for campaigning against conscription. 'In the coming months there is no doubt that the men who rule Washington will try to damage you in every way open to them, but I am sure you know that you spoke for your people and for the oppressed everywhere in the courageous defiance of American power. They will try to break you because you are a symbol of a force they are unable to destroy, namely, the aroused consciousness of a whole people determined no longer to be butchered and debased with fear and oppression. You have my whole-hearted support. This is a war more barbaric than others, and because a mystique is built up around a champion fighter, I suppose the world has more than incidental curiosity about what the world champion thinks. Usually he goes with the tide. You surprised them.' On the day Ali's trial began (19 June 1967) a group calling itself the 'Stop It! Committee' held a sympathetic demonstration outside the London offices of the British Boxing Board of Control. All, of course, to no avail. The American establishment was not about to make any concessions and the government duly exacted its pound of flesh. 'To those of the press and those of the people who think that I lost so much by not taking the "step" I would like to say that I did not lose a thing. I have gained a lot. I have gained peace of mind.' The People's Champion was born.

Although Ali was free to travel the length and breadth of his native land fighting exhibition bouts the only opportunity his British fans had of watching him perform inside the ropes was the bizarre 'Computer Fight' with Rocky Marciano, broadcast by the BBC on the evening of 21 January 1970: 'It's Cassius v Rocky: presenting the heavyweight fight of the century.'

Who was the 'Greatest' of them all? Comparisons, they say, are odious; but they are as enjoyable as they are inevitable. Why not feed the relevant details of 16 champions into a computer and programme it with a series of elimination contests to reveal the answer? Murray Woroner's brainchild was first tested for American radio; Marciano defeated Jack Dempsey in the 'final', Ali having been 'outpointed' by Jim Jeffries in an earlier phase. Ali threatened to sue for a million dollars . . . but settled for one dollar on being offered a filmed fight with Marciano. Over and above the obvious pitfalls associated with putting two undefeated champions into a ring and requesting them to 'act' there was the tiny consideration of The Rock's physical condition. The sight of a pudgy, balding 45-year-old was not conducive to authenticity. $150,000 provided Marciano with the incentive:

green always was a fighter's favourite colour – the colour of money. Marciano shed 40lb and was fitted with a toupee for the 75 one-minute fight segments filmed at Studio City, Miami. The clips encompassed every conceivable scenario and conclusion (seven of them). Five cameras were positioned around the ring but they captured not a single punch. Rocky swung; Ali jabbed; but no glove ever landed. Only three people knew the computer's decision ('more closely guarded than the gold in Fort Knox', declared *Time* magazine) prior to transmission in 1,000 cinemas across America. Before taking his seat in a Philadelphia cinema Ali quipped: 'If I lose, that computer was in Alabama!' The frantic efforts of the commentator were not echoed in the limp action on screen. The grunts and thuds are patently sound effects; the bobbing and weaving could have been choreographed by Fred Astaire; and you could almost smell the tomato ketchup on Marciano's cut eye. Ali saw himself deck Rocky in the sixth with a short right, then go down himself in rounds ten and 12. Worse followed. After 57 seconds of the 13th a left hook to the head sends him sprawling for the full count. The Rock is the 'Greatest'! Ali's verdict? 'It takes a good champion to lose like that! Sure, it upsets me. But it's just fiction, a make-believe fight. People have seen me in the ring for the last time tonight. I will never fight again. The public would like to see me fight

The Rock and The Greatest slug it out for the cameras (Press Association)

but the boxing officials and the politicians haven't got the guts.' It was only fitting that Marciano was given the nod. Three weeks after filming was completed he was killed in a plane crash and went to his death not knowing the 'result'. Ali subsequently denounced the fight's phoniness on nationwide television. The US networks may have craved victory for the 'white boy' but on this side of the Atlantic racial politics were immaterial. The BBC's rights were for delayed transmission only and on learning of the computer's 'decision' the Beeb asked for an alternative ending!

Unlike various boxing authorities some bodies became increasingly keen to anoint Muhammad Ali as one of their own. Ali's grasp of poetry and magic were, it must be admitted, fairly rudimentary but this apparent disadvantage did not prevent his name from being put forward as a candidate for both Oxford University's chair in poetry and membership of the British Magical Society. Ali's poetic adversary was Stephen Spender, endorsed by no less than W.H. Auden; twin advocates of his own suit were Nicholas Stern and Duncan Macleod of St Catherine's College. Stern's case went as follows: 'We are putting Ali forward to show the pomposity of lightweights evaluating senior poets, whose poetry they are not competent to judge. I think Ali has got a good chance but it depends on the good humour of the electorate.' The post, dating from 1708, fell vacant in November 1973 and ran for a period of five years; in return for the honour (and £300 per annum) Ali would be expected to deliver three lectures a year. Ali's reply naturally came in verse:

> Pay heed, my children, and you will see
> While the time's not right for your University.
> Not because of the pay, although it is small,
> It's because I have to show the world I can still walk tall!

And so Oxford University narrowly missed acquiring the talents of a poet quite unlike any other.

Ali's fascination with magic and his obvious delight in its performance were equally well known, prompting the British Magical Society to welcome him with open arms. However, Ali's religious conviction that you should not deceive anyone compelled him to reveal all on completion of the 'trick' – and this was not received so cordially. In May 1984 the Society's secretary, Barry Gordon, reluctantly announced Ali's expulsion from the order. 'When Ali came to Britain several years ago he did a number of magical items on some of his interviews and we decided it would be a nice gesture to welcome him to the brotherhood. Now, however, he has broken the cardinal rule of all magicians by exposing how the tricks are done and we have decided to remove his name from our list of honorary members.'

Ali gave as well as received. As the stricken Michael Watson was to discover in 1992 'The Greatest' would always find time in busy schedules to support a fellow boxer down on his luck. In 1979, for instance, this had involved attending a benefit function for the former British and Empire heavyweight champion Joe Erskine. Says Jarvis Astaire: 'After one of his trips over here Ali left money with me to use in helping publicise and promote anything of this nature. He told me to place adverts in the papers and in fight programmes whenever anything to do with boxing charities came up. He was always incredibly generous. A well-known example of his generosity concerned Teddy Waltham. We had arranged some exhibitions for Ali in Genoa and Waltham, who was getting on a bit by now, refereed on the same bill – it wasn't a Frankfurt promotion, by the way, as has been related elsewhere. Waltham was paid in cash and then promptly got his pocket picked. On the plane back Ali got to hear of this and immediately gave Waltham the exact amount out of his own pocket. When Mickey Duff commended him for doing it, Ali said: "I saw the fight and that man worked hard for his money."' Duff, himself, tells a story of how Ali contributed to a benefit dinner for the one-time British, Commonwealth and European light-heavyweight champion Chris Finnegan, forced to retire with eye trouble in 1976. Ali promised Duff the gloves he would wear in the upcoming title fight with Richard Dunn so they could be auctioned at the dinner. Duff received the gloves immediately the fight ended in the fifth, whereupon Ali told him to look inside them. There in Ali's own handwriting Duff found 'Ali wins' in one and 'KO, round five' in the other!

Few such charity auctions were allowed to pass without some item of equipment bearing Ali's signature. Trunks, boots, gloves, robes; some once his personal property, most not. Ali was ever ready to lend his charismatic weight to a worthy cause. The most incredible of these was a four-day cavalcade through the North-east in July 1977: 'The King comes to Geordieland', as it was described in *Boxing News*.

This extraordinary enterprise was the brainchild of 43-year-old Johnny Walker, a painter and decorator from Whitburn. Once a talented amateur boxer who had won a Golden Gloves title during a spell in the USA with the army, Walker devoted much of his spare time to coaching in local boys' clubs; he wondered whether Ali might be persuaded to raise funds for these hard-pressed centres through a personal appearance. Walker sought the advice of Andy Smith, Joe Bugner's manager, in whose gym he occasionally used to train. Smith told him to buy a plane ticket to Chicago and approach Ali man to man. Funded by two local businessmen, builder Larry Shinwell and scrap metal merchant Jimmy Stanley, Walker flew out of Newcastle airport on 30 March 1977, waved off by Frankie Vaughan, President of the National Association of Boys' Clubs and himself a boxer in his teens. While Walker was airborne Dick Kirkup, privy to the scheme and

Paddy Monaghan presents Ali with a trophy inscribed 'The People's Champion' (Paddy Monaghan Collection)

Monaghan assists Ali in the time-consuming business of answering fan mail (Paddy Monaghan Collection)

The Magic Handkerchief: now you see it, now you don't (Paddy Monaghan Collection)

a journalist on the *Shields Gazette*, alerted the *Chicago Daily News* of his imminent arrival and purpose. 'Mission Impossible' had commenced!

'I'd always had the idea of bringing Ali to the North-east. I'd met him once before, in 1966, when he was here to fight Brian London. I took my young son David down to London to see Ali and the *Daily Sketch* fixed it for him to meet Ali in his hotel. "David meets Goliath" they called it and there was a photo on the front page! We didn't keep in touch afterwards but I never gave up hope of one day getting him to come up here. We were desperate for funds so I set about doing it. I collected letters of introduction and goodwill from everywhere: the Lord Lieutenant of Tyne and Wear, local MPs and a host of boxing personalities; Harry Levene was very kind and gave me a letter. The only one who said I wouldn't even get near him was Mickey Duff. When I arrived in Chicago there was nobody there from Ali. He had gone to Berrien Springs where he had a new ranch. So I went to the *Daily News* and told them my story and it appeared on the front page! They had apparently got in touch with Ali and he read the story. The next thing I knew was my name being called over the hotel tannoy. Four huge seven-foot guys were waiting for me: "Are you Johnny Walker? Muhammad wants you!" is all they said before frogmarching me out to a stretch limo that whisked me off to Ali's house, two hours drive away. Ali

86

The Muhammad Ali knock-out show!

A souvenir of Muhammad Ali's South Tyneside visit

Reporters: Catherine Hansen, Ron Popper and Susan Wear.

When the Champ came to town

MEN, thousands of them, danced saluted, clapped and even blew kisses to their Boys' Own hero, Muhammad Ali, as he made a triumphant entry into South Tyneside.

In carbon copy scenes of the Queen's visit, people perched everywhere from window ledges to the roofs of bus shelters, up lamp posts and along foot bridges.

And although not so many lined the route into South Shields as for the Queen, the welcome was no less emphatic.

In Bede Burn Road and York Avenue, they cheered him all the way.

From the smallest toddler to stick-waving pensioners, it was a smiling, open-mouthed ecstatic welcome. As the open-topped Silver Jubilee bus crawled down Boldon Lane and Stanhope Road to Chichester, the crowds packed tighter forming a sea of green banners outside the Mosque in Laygate.

But the Market Place and King Street scenes were unbelievable. Six and seven deep they stood on both sides of the road but even these crowds were outshone by those at the Amusement Park where Ali was mobbed as he went to collect a £250 cheque for North-East boys' clubs.

As he walked through to the fairground to collect another £250 cheque, he disappeared in a thin blue line of policemen who had to work overtime to keep a path open for Ali.

And they had to do a repeat performance to get him back to the sanctuary of the bus as youngsters and men surged forward regardless of the danger from the moving bus wheels.

★

LEFT: Muhammad Ali's triumphant procession along King Street, South Shields.

'The King comes to Geordieland' (Johnny Walker Collection)

himself opened the door; I showed him the "David meets Goliath" cutting and began explaining to him why I had come, how the kids had to train and fight with no proper equipment or kit – the backsides hanging out of their trunks and no boots. Ali was stuck for words at first. Then he stopped me and said: "You mean you came all the way across the ocean to see me and you didn't call anybody and nobody in my office knows you're coming and you expected me to be at the airport to pick you up? Ever since you've been here you have been talking about helping others. I haven't heard you say anything about yourself. You call yourself poor: you're not poor, you are rich. The things you are doing are going to get you into heaven. Allah must have sent you to get me to help these kids." That evening I sat down to dinner with Muhammad, Veronica and their baby Hana. Muhammad said to Veronica: "Going to England could be part of our honeymoon, couldn't it?" – they were to be married shortly. I was emotionally taken aback. I couldn't get to a phone quick enough to let Jimmy know the news. I stayed for two or three days. We did two TV shows and the press followed us everywhere once the story grabbed public attention. Ali even invited me to spar with him in his gym. My footwork wasn't as good as it was and I failed to dodge a quick jab. It caught me slightly, but even in fun the punch was enough to just nick the corner of my eye. It was nothing serious of course but I always hoped it would leave a little scar so I could show people what The Greatest did to me one day in fun!'

Walker had got his man. 'Ali hears Briton's plea, agrees to aid poor kids', headlined the *Chicago Daily News*. Ali's manager Herbert Muhammad gave Walker a 'tentative acceptance', provided air tickets, ground transportation and accommodation for an entourage of 12 was guaranteed. Ali was more emphatic: 'I don't care what my manager said, I'm telling you right now that I will be there. And when I say I'll be somewhere, I'll be there! My lawyers told Johnny that it would cost at least £15,000 to get me. Johnny told the lawyers that he and the boys club had "nowt" and that he had come to us for money! Lawyers only know money, not affairs of the heart. I am supposed to be training for a serious fight but I'll go because it's a worthy cause and fits in with my religious beliefs. Islam teaches you that you are judged by God on what you do for other people. I want to go to heaven so I have to do these things. I saw God in Johnny's eyes and I had to back him up. Johnny came all the way to Chicago and took a chance of getting me. He convinced me. He told me about his part of the country and how homely the people are. They sound my sort of people and it will be a great honour and a privilege to visit them. Everyone told Johnny he was crazy. I can just hear them now: "You mean you got Muhammad Ali, the champion of the world!" He has made them eat their words. If I was this fellow, an ordinary unknown person, trying to get Frank Sinatra or some other superstar to come all the way to another country, it would be a dream come true.'

Johnny Walker gets his man (Johnny Walker Collection)

The 'dream' was set to come true at 10.55 a.m. on Thursday, 14 July 1977, when Ali's plane touched down at Newcastle Airport. Tyneside has never known a year like 1977: three world figures visited the area. US President Jimmy Carter (along with Prime Minister James Callaghan) had paid a flying visit in May and the Queen sailed up the Tyne in the royal yacht *Britannia* to spend a day on Tyneside on the first full day of Ali's trip. Ali's arrival, however, did not pass without a hitch. His plane was 25 minutes late coming into Heathrow and he was still passing through Customs when the connecting flight to Newcastle took off. 'They should have held the plane if they knew Muhammad Ali was coming,' he joked. 'That pilot is destined for hell! He's British; it's his country. All he had to do for his part in the charity was to hold the plane a little. God's going to say: "Get the fire ready!"' With every other flight to Newcastle fully booked, Ali caught a plane to Teesside and was brought by Rolls-Royce to Newcastle Airport where 17 youth jazz bands energetically set the tone for what turned out to be a hectic itinerary. Ali had already been without sleep for 26 hours; in the course of the next 72 hours he would attend 19 different functions. No wonder he was heard to mutter: 'Man, my feet are killing me!'

After snatching forty winks at his hotel (the Holiday Inn, Seaton Burn) he was chauffeured off to fuctions at the Westend Boys Club and Newcastle

Civic Centre, before finally attending a dinner organised by the Tyne and Wear branch of the Variety Club in aid of the Pendower Special School (for handicapped children) at the Gosforth Park Hotel; waiting for him in the foyer was 12-year-old Ian Pleasant bearing a present of a polystyrene butterfly.

If Thursday had driven Ali to the brink of exhaustion the following day's timetable was absolutely assured to knock the stuffing out of him. First stop was the Pendower Special School in Newcastle's Bertram Crescent, where he passed on a cheque for money raised at the previous night's dinner. The link between Pendower and the boys' clubs was Sylvia Hogarth, the physiotherapist for Community Health Services: 'We were looking for a celebrity to visit the school and the trip organisers were looking for other areas he could align with besides the clubs; and it was a wonderful opportunity to introduce young disabled people to sport. He was charming and related to the youngsters so easily. I don't think he'd come across such disabled kids before and he was so interested in what they did and the sports they liked.' Ali spent an hour chatting to the pupils: seven-year-old Neil Rutter gave him a bottle of aftershave; nine-year-old Darren Cooper handed over a Jubilee mug; Stuart Evans and little Paul Gardner even squared up to the champ, the latter being allowed to land a nifty left hook to the nose. It was a day Pendower has never forgotten and the very mention of Friday, 15 July 1977, to the members of staff who experienced it at first hand brings forth a torrent of colourful memories. Margaret Danskin: 'It was a very busy day because after Muhammad Ali's visit in the morning we were taking 200 children down to the quayside for the arrival of the Queen in the *Britannia*. There was no attempt at lessons that day!' Muriel Oates: 'We thought it would be just a private visit to us alone but crowds of press, TV and radio people turned up and we had to call the police in to control them all. The biggest headache, though, was him arriving late. We had the children in the hall where they were going to welcome him with a song. I was playing the piano and each time a car appeared we started to sing, "If you're happy and you know it clap your hands". The number of times we sang it! We must have gone through our entire repertoire two or three times before he eventually arrived. He was stupendous and he said to me: "When I look at these children and I've got a healthy child it makes me want to cry." He was lovely.' Jean Childs: 'The noise level and the excitement was immense and the children were as high as kites! But Ali was so charismatic; I have to say that the Queen paled into insignificance after his visit.'

Ali's sparring for the day was not yet done. Eighteen-year-old Les Close got his turn at the Grainger Park Boys Club. En route to the club Ali suddenly turned to the coach driver and asked him to stop. The coach pulled to a halt with everyone wondering what was wrong. Ali got out and

Paul Gardner plants a nifty-looking left hook on the champ's nose (Newcastle Journal)

made his way to where a woman was sitting in an invalid chair. He tenderly held her hand, obliged with an autograph and, on his return, said: 'What a beautiful person; you know, she even recognised me.' He was genuinely moved and sat in silence with his thoughts for a while. The main events of the day were a civic reception at Newcastle's Mansion House followed by a seven-course banquet in the Mayfair Ballroom billed as the 'Parade of Champions'. Among the guests paying up to £50 a ticket were many big names in British boxing – Terry Downes, Chris and Kevin Finnegan, Dave 'Boy' Green, Alan Rudkin, Bobby Neill, Howard Winstone and recent Ali victim Richard Dunn, who immediately entered into the spirit of the occasion by stripping off his jacket and threatening to settle an old score. It took a full 20 minutes for Ali to shake hands with all the dignitaries. 'This is some job,' he told the Lord Mayor, Tom Collins. 'Don't you ever get tired standing around like this?' The evening included a two-hour cabaret led by Frankie Vaughan and an auction; a photographic portrait of Ali, Veronica and Hana taken at the Newcastle studios of Turners upon their arrival fetched £1,650 and an autographed pair of white boxing gloves, £1,850. Ali himself returned £7,000 of the £10,000 he had requested to cover his travel and accommodation. Before departing he wrote in the visitors' book: 'Muhammad Ali. Peace, 1977. Service to others is the rent we pay for our stay on earth.'

Saturday proved no less frenetic. It was, according to Ali, 'a day I will

91

(Johnny Walker Collection)

remember until I go to my grave'. It started with a ride through Johnny Walker's home town of South Shields on an open-topped double-decker bus – still decked out in Silver Jubilee regalia, including a large photo of Her Majesty on the front. It was the closest they came to meeting each other on this occasion, although they had met in Washington the previous year. 'Being upstaged by the Queen of England is a big, big honour,' Ali teased reporters. 'Even to be compared to the Queen, me a little black boxer from Louisville, Kentucky, is a big, big honour.' The motorcade wound its way through the streets of South Shields, past crowds ten deep on the pavements, and on to the sea front where a brief halt was called at the fairground. Ali received two cheques, one from Jack Powell on behalf of the fairground and one from Ron Taylor, owner of the boxing booth, before enjoying a ride on the Waltzer. The motorcade's destination was the Gypsies Green Stadium, venue of a carnival featuring all manner of side-shows and stalls. Awaiting Ali was Welsh darts maestro Alan Evans whom he was to 'play' in a novelty match sponsored for £500. Ali won the ten-minute open-air contest! 'I didn't let him win,' Evans wailed. 'A strong cross wind kept blowing my darts out of the board!'

Next stop was the Eldon Square Sports Recreation Centre back in Newcastle for a question-and-answer session with Reg Gutteridge in front of an audience of 900 – part of which went out 'live' on ITV's *World of Sport* programme. The evening's entertainment, however, was for many the highlight of the entire weekend: an exhibition of boxing between past and present champions at Sunderland Football Club's Washington Sports Centre. Ali agreed to box five rounds himself. A crowd of 1,500 saw local fighters Reg Long and Bruce Wells have a round each; Johnny Walker took one himself; while Richard Dunn handled the last two. Terry Downes was the man in the middle. It was laugh-a-minute stuff from beginning to end.

Johnny Walker freely admits to having been swamped by the tide of events that July Saturday. 'Whatever I asked Muhammad to do, he did it. He was marvellous! There was not a person he didn't acknowledge. We were told to take a different route to the Queen's because it might seem Ali had got a bigger turnout. The town was jam-packed. A one and a half hour journey down to the beach took two and a half hours. Ali just couldn't believe that so many people at the other end of the world thought he was The Greatest. It was Dick Kirkup's idea that I went into the ring with Ali. Dick said everyone should see who I was, so I got in with Ali. Well, he went on the deck as soon as I hit him! I wasn't about to let him get one up on me so I did exactly the same when he threw a punch at me! It was super!'

The pace remained unrelenting; Sunday morning began with Ali leaving the hotel clutching a tray from which he was trying to finish his breakfast. He was heading for the Al Azhar mosque in Laygate Lane, South Shields, where his recent marriage to Veronica was to receive a blessing. A path had

South Shields turns out en masse to watch the motorcade meander slowly through the shopping centre to the Sea Front. Ali is flanked by Jimmy Stanley and Johnny Walker (Johnny Walker Collection)

to be cleared through a 7,500-strong crowd (one of whom, 56-year-old Bill Lodge, presented Ali with a crown) so that the couple might enter the mosque for a ten-minute ceremony conducted by Imam Taleb Ahmed. Later on, Ali addressed 1,000 members of Newcastle's Muslim community at the Islamic Centre in Elswick – but only after Veronica had dragged him off for a whirlwind tour of Alnwick Castle: 'My wife wanted to see a castle while she was over here, so we had to visit one!'

The curtain finally dropped on this amazing fund-raising spree on Monday morning when Ali boarded the London-bound Trident. 'I am taking away memories of the most wonderful reception I have experienced anywhere in the world. I never thought it possible for my family to be made so welcome by so many white people. I expect this kind of reception in Africa. It's commonplace there; but to receive a reception like this in a European country! Hearts have no colour; minds have no colour.'

Thanks to Muhammad Ali, boxing in the boys' clubs of the North-east would be rejuvenated by something in excess of £20,000. Peter Mortimer, poet and arts critic of *The Journal*, fittingly put into verse what the Geordies thought of the pugilist and poet who had taken Geordieland by storm.

HOWAY THE CHAMP

To Tyneside you come
with your glory clouds trailing.
You're the Champ of the World
who nobody's failing.
You came bouncing right back
when they said you were fading.
With your butterfly dance
and your sting like a bee,
the Geordies say welcome
to Muhammad Ali.

Muhammad Ali,
you're still on the throne.
Ain't no other fighter
that's ever been known
with a pen and a fist
to match up to your own.
From the earliest days
right through to the latest,
when they talk of The Ring
and they mention The Greatest,

Ali seems to be informing Alan Evans: 'I'm the champion now!' (Johnny Walker Collection)

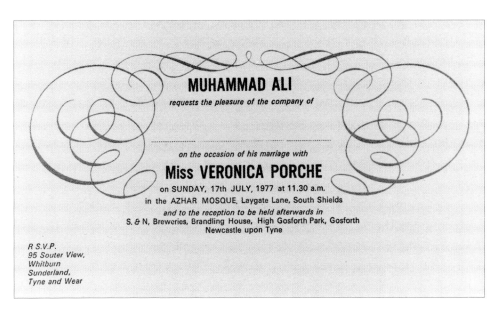

MUHAMMAD ALI

requests the pleasure of the company of

....

on the occasion of his marriage with

Miss VERONICA PORCHE

on SUNDAY, 17th JULY, 1977 at 11.30 a.m.
in the AZHAR MOSQUE, Laygate Lane, South Shields
and to the reception to be held afterwards in
S. & N, Breweries, Brandling House, High Gosforth Park, Gosforth
Newcastle upon Tyne

R.S.V.P.
95 Souter View,
Whitburn
Sunderland,
Tyne and Wear

(Johnny Walker Collection)

there are only two men
who it ever could be.
Cassius Clay –
then Muhammad Ali.

The extent to which Ali had become an icon to diverse sections of society was phenomenal. Forests must have been felled to provide the tons of wood pulp for the plethora of books and magazines devoted to him which his fan clubs (Paddy Monaghan's 'official' fan club subsequently had several imitators) avidly collected. In 1975 a pop record dedicated to him crashed into the British charts. Johnny Wakelin's *Black Superman*, entered the top 20 on 18 January and stayed there for ten weeks, reaching as high as number seven: 'Mu-ham-mad, Mu-ham-mad Ali, floats like a butterfly and stings like a bee . . .'

This idolatry caused Ali occasional concern. In an interview of December 1974 he said: 'I'm not looking to be idolised. I'm not in boxing to be recognised as great in everyday life. I'm The Greatest in the ring but when I come out I'm just a brother, humble like other people, I don't try to be idolised. I don't want to be idolised. You should idolise God and the prophets and the messengers of God. You shouldn't idolise me. You can like me but there's no need to idolise me.'

Millions found, and still find, it impossible to comply with their hero's request. Ealing taxi-driver Ian Parsons was captivated by Ali as a ten-year-old back in the '60s and has built a huge book collection dedicated to him. 'He really is a very humble man when you meet him. When I did in 1986 he gave me a meal and took me to the Bruno-Witherspoon fight.' Perry Aghajanoff was still in short trousers when Ali was in his prime but the 31-year-old Tottenham warehouse manager is now the honorary secretary of the original Muhammad Ali Fan club. 'The '60s and early '70s was a golden age for heavyweight boxing and Ali was the best. He fought everyone. I'm only interested in the best and he was that. The only way to touch the guy was through memorabilia and reading contemporary reports and that is what I did. Paddy was well known in boxing; part of the folklore; a legend in his own right. I kept on visiting him and when he became ill it all fell into place that I should help the fan club. Through Paddy I have met Muhammad. When he came over for the *Ali* show at the Mermaid Theatre we had dinner together and sat next to each other at the performance. Muhammad is up there with the "greats" of all types. In 100 or 200 years time people will look back and be as fascinated by Muhammad Ali as we are by the likes of Mozart.'

ROUND SEVEN

'HE'S TAKEN BOXING AND BROUGHT IT TO A NEW ECONOMIC PITCH'

Barely 11,000 paying customers occupied the Miami Beach Convention Center and St Dominic's Arena in Lewiston, Maine, to witness Muhammad Ali and Sonny Liston dispute the heavyweight championship of the world on 25 February 1964 and 25 May 1965. In stark contrast, over one million fans packed 271 closed-circuit outlets throughout the USA to watch that first encounter at long range. In the UK two million people tuned their radios at 2.55 a.m. to catch the first fight as it happened, while its delayed transmission on television at six a.m. and 8.25 p.m. were watched by an estimated five million and 20.25 million respectively. In Nottingham the unanticipated surge in electricity demand was sufficient to temporarily black out areas of the city; the extra one million kilowatts was said by the Central Electricity Board to be the equivalent of High Marnham power station's entire capacity!

Boxing had embarked upon a new era. The second Ali-Liston encounter was transmitted live to the UK by the Early Bird satellite – thereby breaking new ground for a sporting event. The emergence of a young and extrovert fistic talent had coincided with monumental advances in the sphere of telecommunications. Major fights became funded by the amount of available cinema and television screens rather than the number of seats in the actual auditorium staging the fight. Muhammad Ali was in the process of making the 'live' gate an irrelevance. Within three years of gaining his crown its eighth defence against Ernie Terrell was shown live in Britain, Australia, New Zealand, Ghana, Kenya, Liberia, Nigeria, Rhodesia, Uganda, Hong Kong, Japan, Kuwait, Malaysia, Mauritius, Singapore and Jamaica, in addition to North America – 37,321 were in the Houston Astrodome on 6 February 1967; the worldwide audience easily exceeded 100 times that number.

Ali could put bums on seats like no other, before or since: because of his extraordinary charisma the sport of boxing suddenly outgrew itself. As Jarvis Astaire ventured to suggest at the announcement of Viewsport's plan to show the 1971 showdown with Joe Frazier at 35 British venues (90,000 tickets ranging from £8 to £40): 'This is not just a sporting event but a great event in the world of entertainment.' Only 20,455 (paying $1.3 million) saw

'The Fight' in the flesh; another 300 million watched the telecast around the world, thereby helping the fight gross $20-$30 million. Three years later the 'Rumble in the Jungle' with George Foreman was screened live in 425 closed-circuit outlets in North America plus live or delayed television transmission in 100 other countries; despite its two a.m. GMT start this particular fight netted Viewsport more money than any other. Three of its venues were sold out before the tickets were even printed. 'There's no question that Ali was tremendously influential in the development and success of the closed-circuit phenomenon,' reflects Astaire today. 'I was usually at the fight and supervising transmission but when I was in London it was quite obvious to me that people were coming to see him and only him. In the same way people today will flock to see a film starring Arnold Schwarzenegger or Stallone just because they're in it. After the success of the second Cooper fight everyone wanted to get in on the act but Ali's management always made sure I got the rights to show his fights.' By the time Ali retired in 1981 promoter Bob Arum, Astaire's American counterpart in the closed-circuit department, could state without fear of contradiction: 'He's taken boxing and brought it to a new economic pitch.'

Not one of Ali's 61 contests was shown live on British network television – not even those versus Cooper, London, Bugner and Dunn – thanks largely to the pulling power of his name at the closed-circuit box office. Anyone wishing to follow Ali's fortunes as they occurred made a beeline to the nearest Odeon, or whatever *nom de plume* their local Rank outlet traded under. As both the BBC and ITV discovered to their cost in the summer of 1966 the national networks could not hope to meet the kind of financial demands asked of them by promoters who made them in the safe knowledge that the assuredly greater profitability of closed-circuit transmission was always going to make it the preferred option.

If technology could guarantee the supply side of the equation boxing still had to provide the demand. How and why it did so received no finer definition than that offered by the young challenger during the build-up to his Miami appointment with Liston: '100 per cent will be coming to see me but 99 per cent of them will be coming to see me get beat. They think I talk too much.' Cassius Clay presented entrepreneurs everywhere with something highly marketable. His own generation were eager to see him triumph; the elder generation was desperate to see him get whipped. In February 1964 the latter seemed the most likely outcome of his challenge to Liston. Later on, Ali was wont to describe his opponent's chances as 'slim and none' – which is precisely how the pundits viewed his hopes of toppling the champion. 'A boy is being sent to do a man's work,' stated *Boxing News*; Peter Wilson thought he might last three rounds, though he did not rule out a first round knockout: 'Somehow he looks too gentle, almost too soft for this tough trade. It's all part of a boy turning into a man

Oxford Mail

No. 10,942 WEDNESDAY, FEBRUARY 26, 1964 THREEPENCE

LATE FINAL

KING CLAY: "I whupped that big bear and I whupped him good."

Sonny gets his money after X-rays

EX-CHAMPION WHISKED TO HOSPITAL—SIX STITCHES AND PLASTIC SURGERY

NO FIX SAYS WINNER CLAY

Liston sits tight after six rounds

AMID CHAOS and confusion typical of the man, Cassius Clay won the world heavyweight boxing championship in Miami today, when Sonny Liston did not come out for the seventh round because of an injured left shoulder.

...acclaims the champ

CASSIUS CLAY: "I can beat any fighter in the world," acclaims himself heavyweight champion.

RETURN FIGHT BID BY COOPER

WEATHER FORECAST

TV—Page 4

KING CLAY, "Oh, I'm so pretty," messes up Sonny Liston's outlook towards the end of the sixth round.

Sonny Liston proves his point. His swollen left arm is inspected by a doctor in a Miami hospital. Verdict?—injury to the biceps tendon, which tore the muscle.

Obedient chorus

Hurt before

Liniment claim

BLACK MARKET TICKET PRICES SOAR
By JOHN PARSONS

No bundles

T.U.C. tells Maudling 'Be bold'

News in Brief

Cousins back

For missions

Record for Goya

Tory critics to fight Heath

From our Political Correspondent

ANGRY criticism is expected to face Mr. Edward Heath, Secretary of Industry, when he attends a meeting of Conservative M.P.s tonight to talk about the Resale Prices Bill.

Public interest

Search for wolf is like hide and seek

Makarios asks de Gaulle to Cyprus

Maude out of hospital

Output of cars reaches record in 'slack' month

From our Motoring Correspondent

CARS are coming off Britain's assembly lines faster than ever. Board of Trade figures issued today show that all records were broken in January.

DUKE TO VISIT OXFORD FOR DEGREE

£232,000 fraud by two men court told

How Oxford's paperboys caught up with the momentous events of 25 February 1964 (Oxford Mail)

. . . and you have the uneasy suspicion that the chrysalis period has been rushed too much.' The boxing correspondent of *The Times* concurred: 'Liston to win in three as Clay will run for two, unlike Patterson.' Of 46 boxing writers polled at ringside only three favoured Clay. Eamonn Andrews thought Clay could win. Angelo Dundee, understandably, could see nothing other than victory for his man: 'I knew I was working with an amazing figure, a unique heavyweight with the hand and foot speed of a welterweight and the heart of a lion. And Liston always had trouble with tall guys and anyone with height, speed or awkwardness.' Significantly more unbiased support came from the one and only Rocky Marciano: 'Forget about his cockiness and loud mouth. This boy can fight. He's probably the best combination boxer-puncher around. He's fast and smooth-flowing and his moves are just about right. He's determined and clean-living. He's smart, he's getting good advice and he's following it.' Another significant disbeliever in the Big Ugly Bear's invincibility was Eddie Machen, the only heavyweight to have gone the distance with Liston in five years: 'He ain't the smartest guy in the world, you know. Most of his opponents have choked up. I had no respect for him. I kept calling him names. I cursed him every time I gotta chance. It kept him confused.'

The Louisville Lip saw to it that Liston was well and truly confused long before he even ducked through the ropes. The sequence of events in Miami Beach embodied everything evoked by the famous line at the end of John Ford's classic western movie *The Man Who Shot Liberty Valence*: 'When the legend becomes fact, print the legend.' Liston was baited relentlessly and outrageously. In prose: 'Sonny Liston is nothing. The man can't talk. The man can't fight. The man needs talking lessons. The man needs boxing lessons. And since he's gonna fight me now, the man needs falling down lessons. I'll hit him with so many punches he'll think he's surrounded. I saw him shadow-box the other day and the shadow won! He's too ugly to be champ. He's so ugly that when he cries the tears run down the back of his head. Set the traps! Ah'm going bear-huntin'. I'm the real champ. I don't want to be just the heavyweight champion of the world. I'm gonna be champion of the whole universe. After I whup Liston I'm gonna whup those little green men from Jupiter and Mars. And lookin' at them won't scare me none because they can't be no uglier than Sonny Liston!' And then in verse:

'Clay moves towards Liston
And Liston starts to retreat
If Liston goes back any further
He'll end up in a ringside seat
Clay swings with a left
Clay swings with a right

However, I'd seen something to convince me that all would be well. Amid all the pushing and shoving and shouting, Clay winked at Eamonn Andrews, remembering him from the fight against Henry Cooper.' The Cassius strategy was simple: 'Liston thinks I am a nut; he is scared of no man but he is scared of a nut because he doesn't know what a nut will do.'

What Cassius Clay proceeded to 'do', as he so aptly put it, 'shook up the world' – at least the world of boxing. The odds against him succeeding had been 8/1: the afternoon of the fight an 8/1 shot called Cassius had won the fourth race at Hialeah, the local track! A boy had been sent to do a man's job but he duly accomplished the task.'It's King Clay as he predicted,' a contrite *Boxing News* splashed across its front page. The new champion, meanwhile, was showing traces of the same quality: 'My mouth overshadowed my ability.'

When we got to see the fight at six a.m. (the nation's newspaper boys tended to turn up mysteriously late on 26 February 1964) even the flickering pictures of an embryonic satellite system could not dim the sense of occasion. Harry Carpenter's commentary, full of surprise and wonderment, drove the celebratory candles firmly into the cake. For some, the images and words proved harder to swallow. While sons gloated, fathers cringed. 'Coming to the end of the first round,' sings Carpenter, 'and it's been a sensational first round and Clay has stolen the honours in it. There's the bell and they're still fighting! They didn't hear it. And now he's started clowning again! Making faces for the photographers. This is what he's been doing all through his training.' Round three was a cracker with Clay launching what Peter Wilson described as 'a two-handed sabre attack'. In two separate onslaughts Liston was hit with every punch in the book – jabs, crosses, hooks, uppercuts landed in droves. Carpenter was more prosaic: 'Liston is cut under the left eye! Liston's face is bleeding and he can't stop the punches coming in to him!' Through round four and the drama induced by something – most probably a coagulant being applied to Liston's eye – getting into the challenger's eyes and panicking him into thoughts of surrender; then, the bell for round seven. 'And what's happened?' Carpenter asks incredulously. 'Clay has won! Something has happened in Liston's corner. They are not going on! A sensation to end all sensations! Cassius Clay is the new heavyweight champion of the world!'

He sure was and he was not about to let anyone forget it. Leaping on to the bottom rope, he bawled at the rows of slack-jawed reporters: 'Eat your words! Eat your words!' before, only marginally calmer, he was interviewed in the ring by Steve Ellis. 'I'm the greatest thing that ever lived. I knew I had him in the first round. Almighty God was with me, I've just upset Sonny Liston and I'm just turned 22 years old. I must be The Greatest! I'm the King of the World! Look at me: I don't have a mark on my face. I'm

The Prettiest and I'm The Greatest! I'm a bad, bad man. I shook up the world . . . I shook up the world . . . I am The Greatest!'

Inevitably, the media made a five-course meal out of the return. The BBC paid what now seems the piffling amount of £10,000 to show the fight live via the Early Bird satellite, all of which ensured that Ali – or Clay as he was still referred to – and Liston adorned the cover of *Radio Times*. The Beeb also dispatched Harry Carpenter and a camera crew with orders to film the champion's preparations for a documentary to be aired prior to the fight. Ali was ready and waiting. 'I had a dream that British writers were coming. And here you are! This is a surprise! You're lucky to have this interview, you know.' Ali's mother, Odessa, Angelo Dundee, Bill Faversham and Joe Martin (the cop in whose Louisville gym Ali began boxing) and even the nun in whose library Ali once worked for nine months, all made contributions. Ali concluded his own contribution with a rendition of the *Tennessee Waltz* and – how could he not? – a prediction: 'I have a surprise for Liston this time. My style will be different, my gimmicks will be different!'

Everyone *was* in for a surprise, albeit of the variety boxing could have well done without. Despite losing the first encounter, Liston (who had, in fact, been level according to the referee and ahead on one judge's card) was a 9/5 favourite to win the rematch. The fight was all over in one minute (the official time), one minute 52 seconds (ten seconds after Liston went down) or two minutes 12 seconds (referee Jersey Joe Walcott's version) depending upon whose opinion you cared to take. Nevertheless, whichever way you looked at it the abiding impression was the same. 'If the word fiasco were not in the language it would be necessary to get an Italian to invent it to describe the shortest and stupidest championship match in the history of boxing,' wrote Alastair Cooke in the Manchester *Guardian*; 'A shambling apology for a world championship,' said George Whiting in the *Evening Standard*; 'A fraud on the American nation,' declared Frank Butler in the *News of the World*; 'A shoddy fraud on the public,' agreed Alan Hoby in the *Sunday Express*; 'Liston shames the sport that rescued him from the gutter,' observed the 'Man they can't gag' in the *Mirror* – 'In all honesty I do not believe that particular punch would have knocked me down.' 'The odour of this contest will be with us for a long time,' decided *Boxing News*. One American newspaper refused to print a report, stating: 'Due to the nature of last night's fight the *Journal* feels it does not warrant coverage – don't look for it in the sporting pages.' The eagle-eyed Reg Gutteridge noted that St Dominic's Arena just happened to be situated at the bottom of Lewiston's Skunk Hill. Years later Harry Carpenter continued to express bafflement at the phantom right hand – Ali called it his 'anchor punch' – which ended the contest. 'It was one of the most curious fights I've ever seen. At the time I thought he'd only hit Liston high up on the temple and not hard enough to knock him out. But I'm not so sure now.' Most people could not scream 'FIX!' fast enough. Henry Cooper, for one, vehemently disagreed: 'It couldn't have been fixed. They'd have made it look better. That was no punch Clay landed. It could not have hurt anybody.'

Although Ali's British fans never wavered in their allegiance to the closed-circuit transmissions of his fights the only subsequent opponents to create the same tingling buzz of expectation as Sonny Liston were Ernie Terrell, Joe Frazier and George Foreman. By fighting Liston a second time Ali had flouted an edict from the WBA, who responded by stripping him of their version of the title. Terrell and Eddie Machen were then matched for the vacant crown; Terrell won on points. The two champions were scheduled to meet in March 1966. Terrell, once a sparring partner of Ali, ducked the first date; nor did he endear himself to his former ringmate by constantly referring to him as 'Clay'. By the time the fight was eventually made for 6 February 1967, Terrell had gone five years undefeated, beating along the way Cleveland Williams, Zora Folley, George Chuvalo and Doug Jones. This one had all the trappings of a grudge fight. Terrell: 'Most guys I've fought I've known beforehand or got to know afterwards. I've never had any malice. This is different. I wouldn't care to socialise with Clay in any way.' Ali: 'At the weigh-in I'm going to ask him one question. It'll be just three words. If he gives me a certain answer I'm going to give him the Patterson torture. I'll be talking and punching. When he misses I'll shake my head at him reproachfully and that will go on, me talking and punching, until the ref stops it. There won't be a knockout. But if he gives me the right answer I'll knock him out as quickly as possible.'

A crowd of 37,321 awaited the gladiators in Houston's Astrodome; once again the closed-circuit paymasters cleaned up, with the fight being beamed into every corner of the globe. 'If Terrell has the ability,' ventured Wilson in the *Mirror*, 'this could be a bitter, bitter fight.' It proved that – and more: 15 ugly, brutal rounds punctuated by Ali demanding of Terrell, 'What's my name?' In the sour aftermath Wilson summarised the unsavoury spectacle of the champion taunting his crippled adversary as 'Float like a vampire, sting like a scorpion'. Boxing's Fleet Street conscience went on: 'It is not legitimate to try to break a man's soul and spirit – when you have already half-blinded him, outclassed and humiliated him – with your tongue. For long squalid segments this was one of the most distasteful prostitutions of boxing I've ever watched. The referee never checked Clay, who for at least half the fight was taunting, jeering, sneering, reviling and blackguarding the man he had sworn to torture and humiliate.' Desmond Hackett, Wilson's alter ego on the *Daily Express*, spoke of 'a collision of sheer savagery'.

When television finally provided the visual evidence it was impossible to disagree with the interpretation of Messrs Wilson and Hackett. This was, indeed, a 'grudge' fight with a capital 'G'. 'And now Ali is telling Terrell to fight,' says Carpenter. 'This is when Muhammad Ali is at his least sportsmanlike. "What's my name?" He says it over and over again! "I want to know my name!" These are some of the most astounding scenes ever seen in a world heavyweight championship fight.' By the eighth Terrell had clearly sustained a grotesquely damaged eye and was being ignominiously reduced to a shambling six-and-a-half-foot clown who could neither see to hit nor see to evade. The three scorecards did not lie: 148/137; 148/137; 148/133. Ritual blood-letting on a shocking scale; yet the referee declined to intervene.

Although this brutal exhibition coined gold for both fighter and promoter alike the size of the pot was as nothing compared to the bonanza generated during Ali's 'second coming'. Ali's three confrontations with Joe Frazier, which culminated in the 'Thrilla in Manila' (described by Hugh McIlvanney as 'a kind of requiem for the heavyweight division'), and the 'Rumble in the Jungle' with George Foreman were assured of establishing new records at the closed-circuit box office: 300 million people spread among 46 different countries watched the first Ali–Frazier fight of 8 March 1971, at 337 closed-circuit locations. Thirty-five of them were in the UK, where 90,000 fans followed events at Madison Square Garden aided by commentary from Reg Gutteridge. In the absence of any live radio commentary ticket touts made a killing; £8 tickets for the Leicester Square Odeon were changing hands at £40 in the early hours of Tuesday, 9 March, as the fight time of 4.30 a.m. GMT drew near. For the majority of us a 50-minute BBC television feature at 9.20 p.m. on Monday evening would have to suffice until the delayed network transmission 24 hours later. Not that *Radio Times* carried any such advice: the BBC, apparently, had paid so huge a sum for the rights that everything was being kept hush-hush. Unfortunately for the BBC the morning papers gave the game away! Poor old Harry Carpenter was required to film so many 'previews' he was virtually lost for words when they were going to matter most. To add insult to injury Carpenter was required to personally bring the tape of the fight back to London aboard a freight aircraft which departed JFK in a snowstorm.

Britain's early risers soon latched on to Simon Smith's summary on Radio Two: 'Not a great fight. I got the impression that Frazier won it easily. Clay was so ineffective. Frazier overwhelmed him and why he didn't knock him out I'll never know. The old Clay magic just wasn't there. I saw people leaving before the end and heard the slow hand-clap on one or two occasions.' They certainly vacated the Newcastle Odeon prematurely: all pictures were lost after a crane crashed through the roof! Smith's opinion was not, however, typical. Gutteridge had Ali ahead after eight rounds, for example, while Peter Wilson was one witness who freely attested to the spectacle; he recoiled at the ferocity on view. 'I was perhaps ten yards from the ring apron but a punch to Ali's midriff in round three threw me back in my chair as though I had been skewered through the guts.' In point of fact, Ali had – we were informed – landed 688 punches to Frazier's 388; but as Wilson had so graphically implied, Frazier's, notably that wicked last round left hook which would have sent 999 fighters out of 1,000 straight to rest and rehabilitation (Ali rose at the count of three), were far more eyecatching, considerably more damaging and ultimately more profitable.

Ali would be back. The silver screen yielded 14 further opportunities to relish the alchemy (including revenge over the now deposed champion Joe Frazier) before he locked horns with George Foreman on 30 October 1974. Once or twice every drop of Ali's impudence was necessary to lift a fight from the mundane. During the singularly uninspiring bout with Rudi Lubbers in Djkarta, Ali granted Reg Gutteridge an interview between rounds. 'Could you say something to *World of Sport* just now, Muhammad?' asked the fearless commentator. Came the reply: 'I'm glad my fans in London can see me in my last days 'cos, you see, I'm getting old now. Years ago I would have taken this man in one round!'

Those 'last days' defied any logic imposed by the calendar, of course, and our Reg was on hand to describe the scenes and events at Kinshasa's Stade du 20 Mai when Ali reclaimed his title by knocking over George Foreman. Not that any of his 90,000 intended closed-circuit audience in Britain heard a word: a post office strike in Paris cut Gutteridge's line and Harry Carpenter's commentary for the BBC's delayed recording had to be beamed in via the USA. Some of Carpenter's phrases that night have entered sporting folklore to rest alongside such as Kenneth Wolstenholme's 'Some people are on the pitch! They think it's all over. It is now!' at the conclusion of the 1966 World Cup final. Harry had no sooner convinced us in round eight that 'Ali's getting tired. His arms are coming down. Ali can hardly hold his hands up!' than he was crying hysterically: 'Ali's got him with a right hand! He's got him! Oh, you can't believe it! And he's doing his shuffle! I don't think Foreman is going to get up! He's trying to beat the count – and he's out! Oh, my God, he's won the title back at 32!'

Yet again The Greatest made the boxing media eat its words. 'Is it all over for the People's Choice?' *Boxing News* had asked. 'Foreman power to crush Ali by round ten. The Age of Ali is nearly over.' Henry Cooper was convinced that 'Ali won't be able to kid George'. Ali, meanwhile, had been talking up a storm of which the other George – of the 'Gorgeous' variety – would have been proud. 'If you think I whupped Sonny Liston, you wait till I get George Foreman,' a seated and apparently composed Ali informed *Sportsnight*. Pretty soon, however, all restraint vanished, Ali leapt theatrically to his feet and, jabbing a finger straight into the camera lens, began ranting like a genuine fairground barker. 'George Foreman talks too much. He's ugly; he's pretending he's a true champion. They make me the underdog! I'm gonna show them all that I'm the real champion. There'll never be one like me! All of you people in Britain who rate me as The Greatest, I'm gonna prove I'm The Greatest. This is my last fight. I don't want you to miss it. So please come to the theatres! I'm gonna eat some raw meat! I'm going to train and get ready! I'm gonna chop down some more trees! So please come to see this fight! If you thought it a shock when Nixon resigned just wait 'til I kick George Foreman's behind!'

Nevertheless, confidence in Ali's ability to wrest back his crown was in short supply; Mickey Duff and Andy Smith were among the tiny minority who thought he could pull off one last conjuring trick. Of the British press Harry Mullan proved himself amazingly prophetic by writing: 'I don't believe that Foreman is intelligent enough (in the boxing sense) to change tactics or adapt himself to any new situations.' In the *Sun*, Colin Hart actually tipped Ali to win by a knockout before round nine. Most journalists tried to hedge their bets. They knew it was never wise to bet against Ali extracting another bemused rabbit from his capacious top hat. Neil Allen spelt out the eternal quandary associated with an Ali tilt at the seemingly impossible by promising *Times* readers: 'A sad night for boxing or a red-faced dawn for boxing writers.'

Harry Carpenter introduced the contest as one between 'a man who represents destruction and a man who represents grace and skill and cunning'. Twenty years after the event he smiles at the recollection of what he saw unfold before his very eyes. 'Ali came out and did all the things that everyone said he must not do. He had to run; he had to keep away. He defied all that and came out and did the unexpected.'

Within 30 seconds of the opening bell our incredulous eyes were being rubbed to confirm what they seemed to be telling us. Ali is dancing all right but he is also trading punches, heavy punches. 'They're going to test each other . . . a fight to the finish . . . and that finish may not be far away if they keep this up!' Harry prophesies. If anything, round two sees Ali's tactics become even more outrageous: 'Rope-a-Dope' commences. To anguished cries of 'Get off the ropes! You gotta stick him! Get outta there!' from Angelo Dundee the challenger does precisely the opposite. Ali allows, indeed begs, Foreman to use him for target practice. Massive, swinging blows are aimed at head and body; Ali responds only in spurts; rounds three and four the same. Carpenter wonders how long Ali can go on taking this kind of stick in a battle he reckons is like two men slugging it out on the cobblestones. However, halfway through the fifth the light begins to dawn. Ali hardly throws a punch for two minutes. He's playing possum; taking nearly all Foreman's shots on his arms. 'Is he trying to get Foreman to punch himself out?' asks Carpenter. 'How do you know with this incredible man?' As the

THE FIGHT OF A LIFETIME

VIA SATELLITE

Presented by VIEWSPORT LTD.

SEE IT LIVE
DIRECT FROM MADISON SQUARE GARDEN

CASSIUS CLAY
(MUHAMMAD ALI)
Former Undefeated World Heavyweight Champion

JOE FRAZIER
WORLD HEAVYWEIGHT CHAMPION

MAKE SURE OF YOUR SEAT-BOOK NOW

ON THE NIGHT OF MONDAY 8th MARCH at 2.00 am. Doors open 1.30 am.

Showing at

FINSBURY PARK (Astoria) ODEON	01-272 2224/5
HAMMERSMITH ODEON	01-748 4081
ILFORD ODEON	01-554 2500
LEICESTER SQUARE ODEON	SOLD OUT
MARBLE ARCH ODEON	SOLD OUT
DOMINION TOTTENHAM CT. RD.	01-580 9562
NEW VICTORIA	01-834 5732
BRIGHTON REGENT	0273 25721
BIRMINGHAM (New St.) ODEON	021-643 0815/6
BRISTOL ODEON	0272 26141/2/3
CARDIFF CAPITOL	0222 31316
GLASGOW ODEON (2)	041-332 8701
LEEDS ODEON (2)	0532 30031/2 and 2280
LEICESTER (Queen St.) ODEON	Leicester 27603/
LIVERPOOL ODEON (2)	051-709 0717
MANCHESTER ODEON	061-236 8264/7
NEWCASTLE ODEON	Newcastle 2671
NORWICH ODEON	Norwich 21903
NOTTINGHAM ODEON (2)	0602 47766/7
SOUTHAMPTON GAUMONT	0703 29772/3
WOLVERHAMPTON GAUMONT	0902 26010

BAR LICENCES APPLIED FOR · HOT SNACK SERVICE

How Paddy Monaghan saw 'The Rumble in the Jungle' (Paddy Monaghan Collection)

Muhammad Ali
4-6-91

Paddy Monaghan

and 'The Thrilla in Manila' (Paddy Monaghan Collection)

bell approaches Ali suddenly springs to life and unloads 20 seconds-worth of rapid combinations. Returning to his corner he forestalls any criticism with the night's most authoritative judgment: 'Shut up! I know what I'm doing!'

It is now perfectly easy to recognise round five as the turning point in the fight. Ali's tactics, originally so unfathomable, can now be appreciated. And they are working. Foreman has been sucked into uncharted waters. His last nine fights had not gone beyond two rounds. Yes, both men are tiring. The difference – and it is a crucial difference – is that Foreman is tiring more quickly than Ali. Those incessant clubbing assaults have consumed vast quantities of energy, both physical and nervous. Foreman is conserving nothing for the later rounds. In the seventh he throws 70 punches to Ali's 25. As he slows more openings will present themselves. Ali is keeping him off balance, turning him, goading him. 'Come on George, lemme see you box! You ain't nuthin' but a cissy! You fight like a girl!' Even Archie Moore, one of Foreman's cornermen, is not exempt. 'Be quiet, old man. It's all over!' Ali tells his former opponent.

Foreman appears to have found a second wind in the eighth until a wild left swing is neatly sidestepped by Ali and he ends up hanging pathetically over the ropes in a neutral corner. This grovelling posture symbolises the onset of his personal nemesis. Ali lures him into the opposite corner like a *torero* playing a bull; spins him with a twirl of the cape and sinks the sword – in actuality a flurry of blows climaxed by a left hook and a solid right cross – deep between the shoulder blades. The *corrida* is over. 'He took on Foreman at his own game and he beat him at it. Have you ever in your life seen anything like that!' concluded Carpenter. 'Ali psyched him, outfought him and outmanoeuvred him in his mind.'

Neil Allen and his colleagues in the press pack had to endure an exceedingly red-faced dawn. 'All of you suckers who write for boxing magazines, all of you suckers bow! You made him great, you made him a bad George, you made him a hard puncher! I didn't dance for a reason. I wanted to make him lose all his power. I kept telling him he had no punch; he swings like a cissy! I didn't dance from the second round. I stayed on the ropes and you thought I was doing bad. But it's a beautiful thing for a heavyweight when you make him shoot his best shots and you know he's not hitting you. He was falling, he was missing. I was blocking and pulling back. If you want to know any damn thing about boxing, don't go to no boxing experts . . . come to Muhammad Ali! I am THE MAN!'

It was left to Hugh McIlvanney to put the 'second coming' into perspective. 'We should have known that Muhammad Ali would not settle for any old resurrection. His had to have an additional flourish. So, having rolled away the rock he hit George Foreman on the head with it.'

SHOWBIZ

Was there ever a time when Muhammad Ali was not in showbusiness? It seems not. Right from the moment he latched on to the potential of Gorgeous George's antics it appeared Ali had bridged the gap between sport and the entertainment business without so much as a second thought. However, in spite of the assorted shenanigans at weigh-ins and press conferences, the ringside challenges, promotional work for health drinks, men's cologne (bearing his name), books, cars (Toyota), stage shows, videos, an album of monologues and poems (entitled, naturally, *The Greatest*) or even participation in a couple of full-length feature films, the evolution of Muhammad Ali's showbusiness personality can readily be traced via perusal of three performances on British television between 1966 and 1978.

In the first, the *Eamonn Andrews Show* of 22 May 1966 (the day after the title fight with Cooper), viewers saw a serious, softly spoken young man, someone who had found his God; a personality light years from the loquacious braggart who blitzed the *Sportsview* studio three years previously. Then, on 7 December 1974, we glimpsed, and more importantly heard, another incarnation during the course of what has come to be regarded by many as the most abiding memory of Ali on British television: the second of his four conversations with Michael Parkinson. Certain sections of this programme became deadly serious as Ali held forth on a number of sensitive racial and religious issues. The sportsman/showman was now crossing the divide which would take him deeper and deeper into an ambassadorial role for his people and his faith. Lastly, on Christmas Day 1978, came an extended edition of *This Is Your Life* in which it was intended (this particular 'surprise' was not exactly unexpected) the full array of Ali's talents would be displayed to the viewing public. Ali did not fail us.

It was a young man of bow-tied, soberly demeanour whom Eamonn Andrews introduced to the ABC studio audience and fellow guests Noel Coward, Dudley Moore and the American entertainers Lucille Ball and Rodney Dangerfield on Sunday, 22 May 1966. Shaking Lucille Ball's proffered hand Ali sat down alongside Andrews and folded his arms in anticipation of the opening question.

ANDREWS: Are you annoyed when people still call you Cassius?

ALI: I do not mind the ordinary person in the street. However, on some programmes in America, mainly in the southern states, some of them are rather smart and they seem to be looking for trouble. You know: 'How do you do, Cassius, ol' boy?' I tell them: 'You know my name fellah . . .'

ANDREWS: Fair enough. But let's have a word about the fight last night, Cassius . . .

For all that aura of imperturbability associated with Eamonn Andrews as a boxing commentator and sports broadcaster he was renowned for 'panicking' in a chat show context, frequently shooting himself in the foot in so doing. At this downward volley Coward flinched, Moore ducked an imaginary punch and Lucille Ball feigned one of her mightiest gasps of 'Oh! My goodness!' Ali merely leant forward and corrected Andrews with a whispered 'Muhammad'. The beleaguered host regrouped.

ANDREWS: The fight ended as we knew it would, on a cut eye. But you yourself looked shocked.

ALI: I hate the sight of blood. It's not my nature to just hurt a man once I see blood gushing from his head like that. Automatically I went on the defensive; clinching and holding, hoping the referee would stop it.

ANDREWS: Did you ask the referee to stop the fight?

ALI: I mentioned it but he paid no attention.

Cue laughter; Andrews' face breaks into a nervous smile. Panic over; order is restored. Andrews might not have escaped so lightly had the conversation been taking place ten years on.

Michael Parkinson had already interviewed Ali ('After every fight I rush to the mirror to make sure I'm presentable. A lot of boxers' features change – mainly when I fight 'em.'); shortly after Ali had regained the world title from George Foreman the two met again in London's Mayfair Theatre on Saturday, 7 December 1974. Parkinson's hour-long, late-night chat show had quickly become the best of its kind in the UK. Usually it featured three guests: occasionally the whole show would be devoted to a 'special' larger-than-life guest – John Wayne, Bing Crosby et al. This was another such occasion. *Kojak, Match of the Day* and, at 11.10, Muhammad Ali: a compulsive night of entertainment. Ali was fresh from honing his patter in a one-man show at the Victoria Theatre but tonight's performance would knock that one into a cocked hat. It was riveting stuff.

Would you buy cologne from this man? (Paddy Monaghan Collection)

Parkinson's introduction was brief and to the point. His special guest was, he told us, one of the greatest athletes the world had ever seen and certainly the most remarkable entertainer of our time; he would be a sell

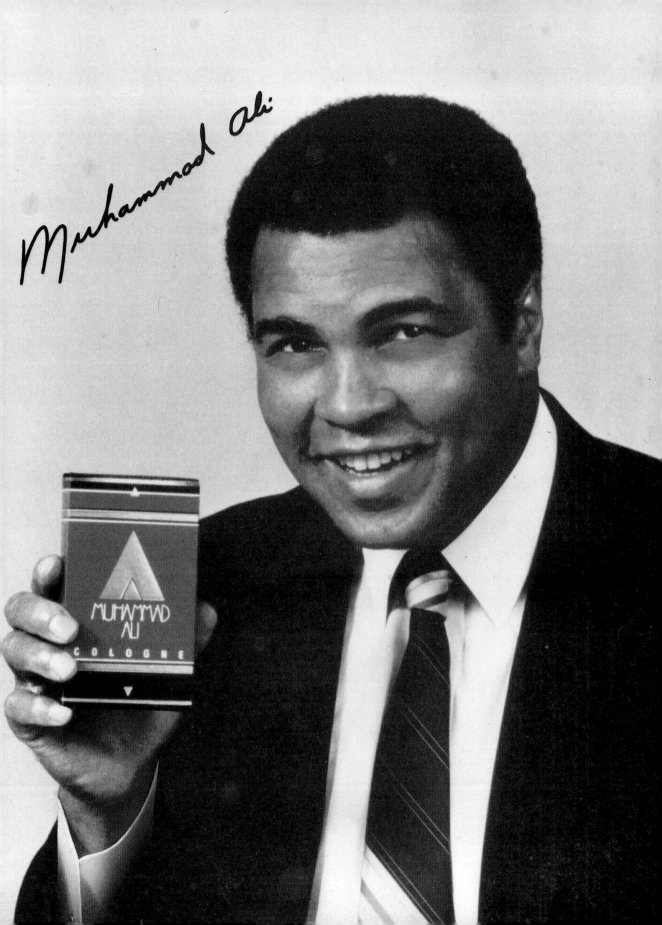

out in Omsk, Ontario or Oldham; his critics would have us think he was arrogant, conceited and a loudmouth; his supporters would claim he is a comedian, poet and a spokesman for his people; the world's undisputed talking champion and beautiful with it. And now back where he belongs at the top of the tree: 'Ladies and gentlemen, the heavyweight champion of the world, Muhammad Ali!'

Ali loped on to the strains of *Black Superman* and eased himself into the green leather armchair deputed for him. It seemed as if Ali had decided to compensate Parkinson for the shortfall in guests by assuming several guises. Guest number one was an old friend to everybody: Ali the Greatest, conqueror of the unbeatable monster, George Foreman. 'All I had to do was to go out and beat one man who had no skill, no class. I don't know why the world was so foolish to believe in him and think that I wasn't going to win. The man fights like a woman; he's wild, no class, no science and he's ugly! I tried to tell them Foreman wasn't nothing.' Then, to demonstrate why he christened Foreman 'The Mummy' Ali assumes a stiff, upright boxing pose and proceeds to slowly circle Parkinson like a poorly programmed robot, moving and punching in mechanical rhythm. The audience roars. 'I should have this show, shouldn't I?'

Next up is Ali the promoter of possible contests. 'I don't like the way you write about Bugner. To put that man down, that's a shame. He must have stole your girlfriend or something. Look, you've got a good White Hope there. You can build the man up, give him some confidence. You should stand up for him; he's your champ. If I want to fight Bugner all I have to do is come here and tell the promoter and they will do anything I say to get it.' With Parkinson thrown on to the defensive Ali rams home the attack by feigning anger and starting to remove his jacket. 'He's scared – he don't know what's going to happen!'

What actually 'happened' was the emergence of a total stranger – at least as far as most viewers were concerned. He began to materialise when Parkinson asked if Ali always wanted to be famous. Yes, he did, and now he wanted to use that position to help his people. The conversation gathered pace and inevitably turned to the differences between black and white culture and Ali's espousal of racial separatism. White culture can corrupt, maintains Ali. He cites western fashions like mini-skirts and hot-pants which are eschewed by Muslim women. 'Horses and cows show their behind . . . Muslim women serve God not some clothes designer . . . If I had a lower IQ I could enjoy this conversation.' At Ali's instigation the camera picks out three Muslim ladies in the audience who are soberly dressed in long robes and head pieces.

Parkinson scents an opening. He produces the book *Loser and Still Champion* written by Budd Schulberg, whom he describes as a 'friend' of Ali. He was not a friend; he was an 'associate', stressed Ali. Parkinson then proceeded to light the blue touchpaper by drawing attention to what he saw as a 'fascinating' contradiction, to wit Ali having many white friends, such as Angelo Dundee, yet espousing a faith that taught racial separatism. 'They are not friends, they are associates,' insisted Ali. Parkinson would not relent: 'You don't have any white friends?' he railed. The flame finally reached the powder; the fireworks began.

According to Ali the white man of America was the blue-eyed, blond-headed devil and the Muslims in America were clean, respected people who just wanted to rule themselves. 'It's a fact that white people hate black people.' At Parkinson's contemptuous dismissal of this hypothesis Ali seemed to bridle. His fervently held beliefs were not being given due respect; he was being patronised. 'You do not have enough wisdom to corner me on television. You're too small mentally to tackle me on anything that I represent. I'm serious – you and this TV show is nothing to Muhammad Ali and if you've got some more questions, I'll answer them and I bet you I'll eat you right here on the air. It ain't no way you can tackle me. All of you are tricky, that's how your John Hawkins, a white Englishman, tricked us out of Africa and America. You get me on your show and ask me all kind of tricky questions . . . Budd Schulberg says you got white men working in your camp and you teach that the white men are devils. How are you going to trap me? You're a white man and your knowledge ain't nothing to a Muslim. How you going to get me on the TV and trap me? Ain't no way. You can't beat me physically nor mentally. You are really a joke. I'm serious, this is a joke. You can read this damn book all you want. I didn't know you had a book waiting for me and were going to ask me all this. Behind stage you're so nice. And we have a nice talk, then you get me on TV . . . this is a serious thing you got with me. You are contradicted, you're attacking my religion.'

Phew! Did we not positively tingle with the electricity crackling from the television set? Enough power was being generated to light up a small city! Parkinson is speechless and palpably shell-shocked by Ali's vehemence. Conceding defeat he takes a deep breath and changes tack. Schooldays; alternative careers – movie acting, perhaps? However, reference to black exploitation movies again raises the temperature and leads the conversation back to racial disharmony. Should not Ali be using his fame to encourage unity between black and white? No! The first priority is to unite all black people because as yet they are not together. 'Your thing is to get me on this show, ask me something that I can't get and have me look like I can't represent myself and what I believe. But you can't do it. I'm a little too wise for you.'

Parkinson defuses the situation by getting Ali to contemplate the day when he would concede his title to a younger man. 'I don't see nobody on the horizon . . . I'm not fighting for me . . . Muhammad Ali's starting to fight for the freedom of the black people.' As the show judders to its conclusion the harassed Parkinson surrenders unconditionally and admits to having enjoyed being on Ali's show. 'I admire you for letting me on your show,' replies Ali, 'and if you show this I'll admire you more!' That said, he makes as if to dash straight out of the theatre.

Back in the sanctuary of his dressing-room Parkinson felt he had handled the interview very badly. 'Ali's performance was by turn funny and angry, lucid and ranting, intelligent and downright barmy. To be frank, I didn't know what to do. I was as confused and wrong-footed by his performance as poor old George Foreman had been a month or so earlier. I think it was the sight of the book that did it. Ali was at best semi-literate and I think he imagined I was going to challenge him to read the evidence. He accused me of trying to trick him, of mocking his intelligence. In any event he went potty. I remember thinking: "How do I get out of this?"'

The programme's closing credits had scarcely rolled off the screen before the BBC switchboard was ablaze with calls from viewers protesting that Ali had been stirring up racial hatred. 'Frontal interviewing of Ali, whether for television or the printed word, was long ago shown to be largely meaningless,' commented Hugh McIlvanney in the *Observer*. 'The clip-board approach elicits either the familiar stage act – the boastful raillery, the jokes and doggerel and outrageous prophecies or finds him obsessed, apparently to the point of hysteria, with one theme, probably that of the Muslim creed and black separatism. It is profitless to draw broad conclusions from such interviews. His rantings on the race issue during the Parkinson show may have indicated the release of one of the powerful currents in his nature, but it is going too far to suggest that here the camera was at last exposing the inner soul of the man, that beneath all the hypnotic charm there burns the destructive intolerance of a black zealot . . . the only way to convey any accurate sense of Ali is to hang around him for a while, to observe and eavesdrop on his life and dip into his sometimes sparkling, sometimes muddied, stream of consciousness.'

Monday's newspapers carried headlines like 'Why Ali blew his top on TV' and quoted Parkinson as saying: 'What do people expect? Ali is the number one spokesman for the Black Muslim movement. People here have the wrong idea about him. He can be very funny and wonderfully entertaining but he is not a chocolate-coloured coon. He is a very committed, fanatical member of his movement and it seems that people don't want to hear some of the things he believes in. On Saturday for the first time he lost his temper on TV. He wasn't playing this time – this was for real. I decided to let him go on and gradually he defeated himself. He was very angry for a while. But there was no question of any incitement to hatred or violence. Anyone who listened carefully would have understood what he was getting at. There may be many people who do will change their view of Ali but I hope to remain his friend.'

Paddy Monaghan, who was a member of the audience, recalls the evening differently. 'You hear a load of silly rubbish; that Parkinson annoyed him because he wanted Ali to read from this book and Ali couldn't read. He was reading the Holy Qur'an every day, word for word, at that time so I'm sure we can quash that story of him being unable to read. He's always in charge of the situation, he's the last person in the world to lose his temper. He'll put people in their places but he certainly wasn't on the edge of his seat shouting and yelling. He was always in control. He would always think of what he was saying before opening his mouth. We were laughing and joking in the car afterwards. He was fine. He never lost his rag. It was good publicity for Parkinson and the BBC. What actually happened was that Muhammad had an urgent meeting back home and was in a hurry to leave the next morning.' (The appointment Ali was anxious to keep was indeed an important one: President Ford had invited him to the White House. Meeting presidents was nothing unusual for Ali; he and Ford met again on 8 July 1976 at a Washington reception for Her Majesty the Queen. 'I've met people the Queen would like to meet,' Ali said irreverently as, waiting to be introduced, he sat with his leg – still bruised from the ill-advised 'fight' with Japanese wrestler Inoki – raised on a chair.)

Ali talked with Parkinson on two further occasions. 'He was a great entertainer, the most remarkable athlete I ever encountered and a fascinating man – and because of his talent as a sportsman and a human being his decline is the saddest story of them all. When I first interviewed him in 1972 the eyes sparkled, the feet twinkled and you could hear his brain whirring. He was smart, beautiful and funny. In the next ten years or so I interviewed him three more times. On each occasion there was a change. The athlete flogging tickets became the zealot selling religion, the child became a man, but always, no matter how he tried, he couldn't stop the humour glinting through. He was a performer and he loved to dance. Then he had one or two fights too many and when we last spoke, in 1981, the light had gone from his eyes, that wonderful expressive face was a motionless slab and he seemed slow and cumbersome. He had become what he believed he would never be – a casualty of the fight game. He told me an anecdote and three minutes later repeated the same story. Since then the reason for the decline has become a matter of speculation and provokes the debate about the dangers of boxing. If it can happen to those the gods truly blessed what chance have ordinary mortals?'

The 1970s were marvellous times for fans of Muhammad Ali – whatever their nationality – but for the British variety the decade was especially so because our idol was frequently among us in one form or another. Once Ali was reunited with his passport he was in great demand for worldwide promotional work. The Ali Roadshow was soon up and running. In October 1971 – only a month before he was due to fight Buster Mathis in Houston – he flew into Britain to endorse a new health drink marketed by Ovaltine (according to Paddy Monaghan he had no idea what the product was). As he travelled from one supermarket to another the crowds grew larger and larger. At Tesco in the Arndale Shopping Centre in Stretford, Manchester, the throng numbered 2,500, and in the crush a plate-glass door was smashed to smithereens. The planned visit of two hours was cut to half an hour. 'Not even the magical footwork of Ali,' opined the *Manchester Evening News*, 'could get him out of such a tight corner.' Ali later described the mayhem to Reg Gutteridge: 'These old ladies – there must have been hundreds of them – pushed me up against a wall asking for my autograph. One policeman appeared and they all stood back. If that had been back home the dogs and the whips would have come out!'

Later on there were books and films to promote. His autobiography, *The Greatest*, written in conjunction with Richard Durham, was published in 1976, necessitating a visit in March. The following year he returned for the 12 August premiere of the cinematic version at the Empire, Leicester Square. At the beginning of the decade *AKA Cassius Clay* also featured Ali on the big screen. Neither film was critically well received but a four-hour mini-series for television entitled *Freedom Road*, in which Ali played a former slave who fights in the Civil War, resulted in a much more favourable response in 1979. In between the commercial obligations Ali invariably found time to meet the people – his people. During the 1974 *Parkinson* trip this entailed a visit to Tulse Hill Comprehensive School in south London. Having been introduced by the Chairman of Governors, Paul Stephenson, he promptly demanded the tallest boy in the school should step forward: 16-year-old Tony Sibbliers duly complied, whereupon Ali tore off his jacket and initiated a bout of sparring. Ali concluded: 'I like your scene, Mr Stephenson, I admire your style. Your pay is so bad, I won't be back for a while.' This couplet became a familiar refrain as it routinely wrapped up scores of Ali personal appearances. Only the victim's name changed: Frank Bough, David Coleman and, most notably, Harry Carpenter, were consistently on the receiving end of this pay-off line which capped Ali's traditional Christmas message to his British fans on BBC television's *Sports Review of the Year* programme.

The first of these bravura performances came in 1966. A stern, straight-faced Ali took the opportunity of demonstrating the 'Ali Shuffle' – from the side; from the front; in close-up, though not in slow motion. 'I have something I would like to introduce to the people there in Britain, all of my British fans. I know many of you have read about and have heard, and if you saw the Williams fight you'll have seen me reveal, the "Ali Shuffle", my new dance for the world. This "Ali Shuffle" is something that's sweeping the nation. Throughout America – young people, ladies, men, all throughout the colleges – everywhere that I've toured since the Williams fight, they're trying to do the "Ali Shuffle". I'm moving and moving and jumping around and just before you know it, just as soon as you do that shuffle, a split second right after that shuffle, is a good punch!'

Not once did the faintest glimmer of a smile threaten to undermine the champion's impassive visage. Back in London the audience was beside itself with laughter. The tone had been set. Ali's audio-visual Christmas card seldom strayed far from a tried and tested formula. The card he was required to play was the Joker; his brief was to entertain. His straight man was invariably Harry Carpenter; his stooges inevitably those 'false' champions of the world, Joe Frazier and George Foreman.

In 1972 Frazier was the object of Ali's barbs: 'He's too ugly to be the world champion. Joe Frazier is so ugly his face should be donated to the Bureau of Wildlife. That man can't write no poems, he can't predict no rounds! I'm not conceited, I'm just convinced! I'm so modest I can admit my own faults. And my only fault is I don't realise how great I really am!'

Twelve months later Foreman, who had won the title by demolishing Smokin' Joe inside two rounds, became the butt of Ali's jokes: 'George Foreman is good and he's strong and he hits real hard but before he hits you he draws his fist back and he warns you. He says: "I'm getting ready

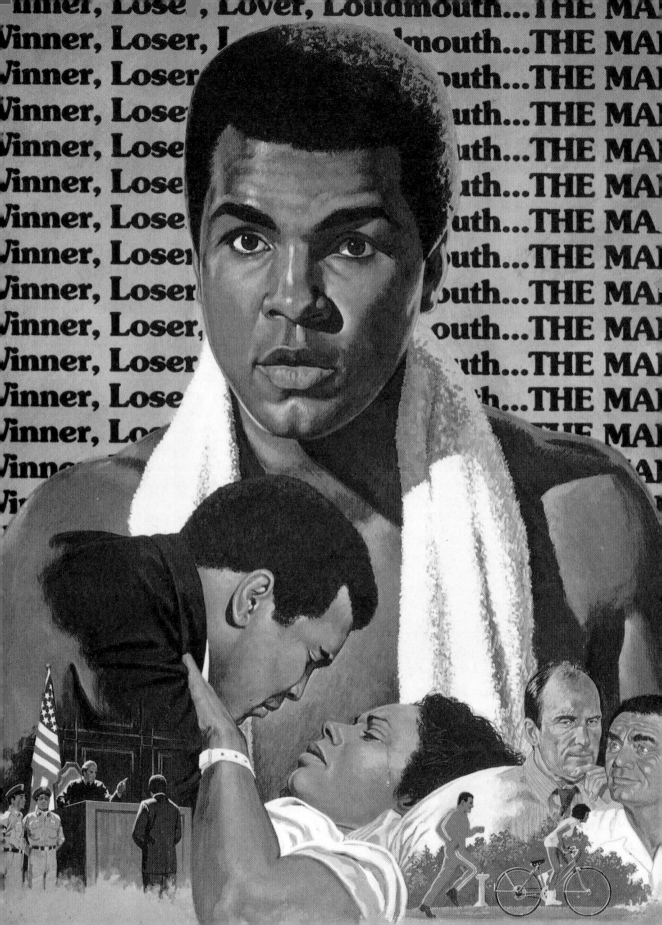

to hit you with a right hand." Someone told me George Foreman was awful strong. I told him he should try a deodorant!'

When Ali won the Overseas Personality of the Year award for an unprecedented third time, in 1978, after he had regained the heavyweight championship of the world from Leon Spinks, the BBC sent Carpenter to Natchez, Mississippi, to present the trophy in person. 'I see my name's not on it like before. That means you didn't expect me to win it!' says Ali in mock sulk which reduces his visitor to a fit of the giggles. The fun was not over. The pair sit and chat on a breezy patio. 'Let me cancel this wind,' says Ali. 'I think I can stop it.' With a half-smile tugging at the corners of his mouth he extends both arms toward the heavens, pauses for effect and then executes a conjurer's flick of the wrists. 'There it goes!' The wind momentarily drops. Ali returns to the conversation. It's time to let us in on a secret. 'I want all my fans out there in Britain to know, if you want me to stay like I am don't wish for me to fight again. It will be hard for me to top that last fight, draw a bigger crowd or make a better fight, the first man to win the title three times. I announce to you in London that I'm never fighting again. But I'm deceiving the American press! I'm tricking them! I'm telling them I might fight again. That way they can't take my title. If I say I'm through completely they'll take my title and give it to some bum! I'm going to get all I can out of it!'

However, ITV had something even more extra special in mind for Christmas Day, 1978: an extended 45-minute edition of *This Is Your Life*. In its long history the programme has frequently capitalised on Ali contributions to enliven proceedings: Messrs Cooper, Carpenter, Andrews and Gutteridge, for example, while even Olympic 100 metres gold medalist Alan Wells somehow became a beneficiary. The *raison d'être* of *This Is Your Life* is that it should come as a surprise to the subject. According to the *Louisville Courier*, Ali knew what was happening before he flew to London; moreover, it declared, he had asked for a fee of $50,000 and forwarded a list of 12 people he wanted on the show – all of whom eventually travelled over on the same aircraft as himself! The programme was recorded on 19 December at the New London Theatre where Ali was ostensibly heading for an interview with Reg Gutteridge. 'I was with him in the car going to the theatre and I'm sure he knew. He was rehearsing what to say! They had Joe Martin on, the cop who first taught him to box. "Get him to ask me about my bike," he said. This bike had been stolen from him as a kid. Come the programme and as soon as Martin says, "Do you remember having your bike stolen?" Ali gasps: "You haven't found it, have you?", and falls on the floor laughing. You can't win with Ali. He can change from a whispering, seemingly bored person to an irrational, angry zealot in seconds. Tricking and putting-on is a natural desire and all part of the fun for Ali. There is a lot of boy in the man. But he is totally genuine. Money he

Poster for the 1977 movie The Greatest *(Paddy Monaghan Collection)*

Ali is besieged in Tesco's supermarket, Stretford, as he tries to promote a new brand of Ovaltine on 14 October 1971 (Mirror Syndication International)

just gives away. I was with him one day in Kuala Lumpur – for the Bugner fight – when he overheard a waitress saying how much she missed not seeing her brother who was in Los Angeles. Ali turned to one of his group and said quietly: "Get her an air ticket to LA. She would like that." I'm very fond of him.'

So despite Eamonn Andrews producing the famous red book with the words 'I'm going to do my best to knock you out with some great surprises', the show probably contained precious few as far as Ali was concerned. All the obvious guests materialised – parents, Joe Frazier, Henry Cooper, Joe Martin – plus Ali's very first opponent, Ronnie O'Keefe (now working in a Ford motor plant), whom he beat on a three-round split decision in 1954, aged 12 and weighing 89lb; and his Polish adversary in the Olympic final, Zbigniew Pietrzykowski – which was a surprise. Film of Waddell's Barber Shop on Louisville's Dixie Highway, where Ali's aunt Eva was a cutter, preceded her 'surprise' entry; film inserts came from Anthony Quinn, who recalled getting into the ring with Ali during the making of *Requiem for a Heavyweight*, and a poignant clip from Joe Louis.

There were also birthdays to celebrate. On 16 January 1979, Ali attended the Classic Cinema in London's Haymarket where a film record of his recent mission to Bangladesh was being shown to the pupils of Acton Green Middle School. In honour of Ali's 37th birthday the following day a splendid cake and a full-throated rendition of *Happy Birthday* topped the occasion. In May 1984 he was the special guest at a 50th birthday party for Henry Cooper. This 'bash' at the Hilton Hotel, hosted by Harry Carpenter, was filmed for television. The event included speeches and a cabaret which necessarily threw the spotlight full beam upon the night of 18 June 1963. The footage of THAT punch was screened yet again; Cockney singing duo Chas and Dave performed a specially composed ditty entitled *Put the Lip to Kip*; while Eamonn Andrews relived the occasion in verse. Then Carpenter invited Ali to join him on stage. Sat opposite each other on a large sofa the Carpenter-Ali double-act went like this:

CARPENTER: You have been as close to Henry Cooper as most people. What do you most remember about him?
ALI: He hits hard! I tell people, it's a funny thing but Henry hit me so hard he jarred my kinfolk in Africa! I was really so lucky because as soon as he hit me the bell rung and I had time to recuperate.
CARPENTER: Otherwise? What would have happened otherwise?
ALI (*diving sideways into the arm of the sofa*): Zzzzzzzz!

On what was obviously an emotional occasion for Henry Cooper this sparkling repartee stole the show. 'This was, for me, the treat of the whole day. What I felt was so good about it was that Ali had accepted the

Even Tom Jones is reduced to the role of fan after joining Ali in a workout (Paddy Monaghan Collection)

invitation and flown over from Los Angeles for the party knowing full well that it would be like putting his head into an opponent's training camp. There at the Hilton he would run into a very British audience – the cream of our showbiz people, sportsmen and commentators, all celebrating MY birthday and recalling the big moments from MY career. At least two of those big moments had to do with Ali, sure, and he could always be secure in the knowledge that he had won both of our fights. All the same, what this audience really wanted to see and cheer about was the time when I knocked him over with the left hook in the fourth round at Wembley in 1963. People had been going on about what a nice man I was, and saying all these kind things about my work for charity but I reckon that in Ali the audience were looking at one of the most remarkable men they were ever likely to see in person in their whole lifetime.'

However, around this period it became increasingly difficult to ignore Ali's physical deterioration. Someone as familiar with Ali as Cooper is able to chart this decline with sad precision. 'I would be lying if I didn't admit to being shocked by his appearance. There was a slur to his speech, he had the movements of an old man and there were times when he could hardly keep his eyes open. He had three fights he shouldn't have had at the end and that's where, I think, the damage was done. He was always so clever at making punches miss; he took punches on the back of the head because he was so clever and perhaps that killed cells at the base of his neck. His deterioration was noticeable. We shook hands in the ring in 1986 before the Bruno-Witherspoon fight; and then even within the 12 months that separated the charity dinner I organised in June 1992 and the *Ali* stage show the following summer I could see a slight deterioration. He would put his right hand in his pocket to stop it shaking, for example. But every now and again he still amazed everyone. At the *Ali* show he actually got up on the stage and did the "shuffle"! After the first fight we got on well enough and I always get a bear-hug from him now. Once the microphones were turned off, notebooks put away and the cameras pointed in a different direction he became quietly spoken and a really nice bloke to be with. He is slower now and he doesn't speak with the old sharpness but there is still that glint in the eye, and the confidence that goes with knowing you are one of the all-time greats of sport. Ali was up there with the presidents and kings for instant recognition – and was more popular than any of them.'

Reg Gutteridge, too, could not help but notice the difference in Ali as the 1980s unwound. 'There were no signs of his health deteriorating when they did *This Is Your Life* in 1978. It started after the Holmes fight in 1980. I don't know of any other boxer with the same plight. I'm sure there's more to it than boxing being the total cause, although he did allow himself to be hit more than necessary in both his training and his fights. In October 1989 he visited me in hospital. He was over here with Frazier and Foreman to

Direct from New York
The Mermaid Theatre
is proud to present
Eric Krebs'
Off-Broadway Smash Hit

ALI

**A Tribute
to
Muhummad Ali
'THE GREATEST'
sporting legend**

starring
GEOFFREY C. EWING

by
**GRAYDON ROYCE
& GEOFFREY C. EWING**

boxing choreography by
RON LIPTON

directed by
STEPHEN HENDERSON

**LIMITED
SEASON
10 JUNE-
13 JULY**

'A KNOCKOUT'
New York Daily News

'A smashing slice of Americana'
New York Post

**REDUCED PRICE PREVIEWS
10, 11 JUNE
PRESS NIGHT 14 JUNE(7pm)
Evenings 8pm
Matinee Saturday 3pm
(no perfs 12 June)**

071 344 4444

MERMAID THEATRE
PUDDLE DOCK BLACKFRIARS LONDON EC4 (Restaurant and bars available)
FOR TICKETS CALL 071 344 4444
or 410 0000 for further details of the new season

promote the *Champions Forever* video and they did the *Wogan* show at White City – Joanna Lumley was actually doing it that night. I was in Hammersmith Hospital with blood poisoning and, when he was told, Harry Carpenter brought him down to see me. I wasn't being allowed visitors but Harry left him at the door and you can imagine what the nurses said! He stayed half an hour.'

Paddy Monaghan noticed a slight slurring in Ali's speech after the second Spinks fight in 1978: 'One of his eyes also screwed up a bit now and again; but I didn't think anything of it. He's told me that if God had allowed him to speak as he used to years ago he would do: it's God's will. It bothers other people more than it bothers Muhammad. He's the same Muhammad as a person. I've got to stay on my toes just as I did 25 years ago; he's forever pulling pranks and joking. I judge a man by his deeds not by what he says. He doesn't say a lot on TV or radio or to the press these days but privately we laugh and talk and joke just like always. Another thing is that we all age and his fans expect to see the same Muhammad Ali they saw 20 or 30 years ago. You can't beat Father Time! Age catches up with us all. He's not the same in stature but people expect him to be. Yet the guy hasn't got a wrinkle on him!'

Jarvis Astaire also testifies to the continued sharpness of Ali's mind. 'Although he may move slowly and speak in a low voice nowadays his mind is very clear and he is as witty as ever. I never noticed any deterioration when he was boxing. It's too easy to just ascribe his illness to boxing. It may well have something to do with boxing but the general view at the time he was fighting was that he didn't get hit too much. A friend of mine had Parkinson's and showed identical symptoms to Ali. And, I believe, Ali's father also developed Parkinson's disease. I still see Ali at the big sporting events, like the Superbowl for instance, and he receives more attention than anyone. If you see a crowd suddenly form round a car you can bet it is Ali arriving! He really is a legend. I'll give you another example. One day I flew into Los Angeles from Australia and when I arrived at the Beverly Hills Hotel Ali was in the lobby talking with John Brown, the Governor of Kentucky, Ali's home state. Ali greeted me with his customary huge bear-hug. Also in the lobby with a group of people was Don Getz, a friend of mine from the film business. So I introduced him to Ali. Two days later Don Getz phones me and says: "My friends were so impressed that I was friendly with a man who was a friend of Muhammad Ali!" That's how much a legendary figure Ali has become.'

Ali's health has ensured that recent visits to these shores have stressed presence at the expense of performance. Even a muted Ali, however, could still upstage Messrs Frazier and Foreman. At their London Arena press call in 1989, Foreman's cry of 'Champ, you were The Greatest!' was met with 'Right! Just what I told you to say. Cost me £5!' Subsequent trips have related to two books – *Muhammad Ali: His Life and Times* by Thomas Hauser (June 1992) and *Muhammad Ali: A Thirty-Year Journey*, a photographic memoir by a long-time friend Howard Bingham (November 1993). In between was a flying visit on 16 June 1993 for the opening night of the stage show *Ali*, a two-hour, one-man *tour de force* at London's Mermaid Theatre, performed and co-written by American actor Geoffrey C. Ewing. Although the critics expressed a degree of dissatisfaction with the play as a whole – 'something of a dud/a pretty routine trudge through Ali's life' – Ewing's ebullient 'impersonation' deservedly won considerable praise.

But, once the 'main man' got up on the stage to perform the 'shuffle' a tumultuous reception left no doubt which 'Ali' had stolen the show – and the heart.

BOXING NEWS
World's Premier Fight Weekly
BIG SHOWDOWN IN PARIS MAY END EARLY
CAN BOONE
JUMP JOE'S
PLACE IN
HOPE MEETS TOP CAT ON NEEDHAM BILL

THE FIGHTS THAT GOT AWAY

Henry Cooper's conviction that everyone 'earned' when they fought Ali neatly summed up all the motivation any heavyweight required in the 15 years following 1966. Fame and glory: glory and money. Understandably, there was no shortage of Britons in the queue. Where Cooper and London had dared in the 1960s Messrs Bodell, Bugner, McAlinden, Dunn and Gardner aspired to be in the 1970s. Not all of them made it to the bank, but it was not for want of trying; and the two who did were obliged to join the Ali circus and enter the Big Top wherever it happened to be pitched at the time – which meant, alas, that a British ring never provided the setting for an Ali fight after 6 August 1966.

The onset of a new decade heralded the departure of an ageing Henry Cooper from the British heavyweight scene. With the man who had ruled the division for so long finally knocked off his pedestal a period of uncertainty ensued in which pretenders to the crown were many and varied. It was 21-year-old Joe Bugner who actually deprived Cooper of his titles on 16 March 1971, and sent the 36-year-old veteran into retirement (Bugner had also 'retired' Brian London in May 1970) but he promptly lost them six months later to Jack Bodell, at 31, a survivor of the Cooper era. This dogged southpaw had briefly been British champion in 1969 when Cooper relinquished the title in protest at the BBBC refusing to sanction a planned challenge for the WBA version of the world title held by Jimmy Ellis, Ali's former sparring partner. Bodell's reign failed to survive one defence. On 27 June 1972 a second up-and-comer, 24-year-old 'Dangerous' Dan McAlinden, a Coventry-based Ulsterman, pummelled him to defeat in a two-round brawl – the pair spent as much time going through the ropes as they did fighting within them – reminiscent of a 19th-century prizefight or the action inside a fairground boxing booth. McAlinden, in fact, had commenced his pro career by defeating three opponents in one night to win a novices competition. Even before he took Bodell's British title his manager, Jack Solomons, had been talking of him fighting Ali – if things went according to plan – in the summer of 1972 at Villa Park, Birmingham. 'This would be nonsense, the biggest mismatch since Bodell met Quarry,' opined Henry Cooper on television, with reference to the most recent instance of a British heavyweight being thrown to the American lions. Inevitably, Ali joined in: 'I want "Macmillan",' he announced after

Who have you British got lined up for me now? (Sport & General)

defeating Jurgen Blin in December 1971, a slip of the tongue which spoke volumes about the credibility of this latest 'potential' British challenger. Thankfully, things did not go according to plan for McAlinden; he lost in eight rounds to an average American called Larry Middleton and the high point of his summer was the meeting with Bodell. Much as Harry Levene ordinarily might have chuckled at the machinations of Solomons being well and truly scuppered, he was in no position to profit from the misfortune of his rival promoter. Neither hopeful in his own promotional camp – Bodell and Bugner – were possible recipients of Ali's largesse in the summer of 1972. Bodell wisely retired after the McAlinden debacle and Bugner was recovering from a broken jaw sustained when he had lost to Middleton in November 1971. The big summer pay-days passed to Jerry Quarry (who got his chance after beating Middleton) and Al 'Blue' Lewis. The latter contest, on 19 July, almost made it to Britain: Ali and Lewis fought at Croke Park in Dublin. And Bugner did manage to get a slice of the action. As part of his rehabilitation he sparred with Ali.

So long as he kept winning, Bugner's chance of donning the gloves for real was never going to be long delayed. In his quest for the world title Ali was prepared to fight everyone. Once Bugner regained the European title by knocking out Blin in October 1972 the hype began in earnest. All that remained in order to set up a 12-round Las Vegas clash on 14 February 1973, was for Bugner to retain his status by defeating Rudi Lubbers. 'A dismal, boring points win', in the words of *The Times*, ensured that Bugner could book his plane ticket and savour the prospect of a cheque for $125,000. Around 1,300 of his fans (plus Henry Cooper who went along to lend moral support) paid £200 apiece to fly over for the festivities, while a further 30,000 reserved seats in 16 British cinemas to watch the closed-circuit transmission. 'Bugner can make Ali hustle', declared an optimistic *Boxing News*; Vegas bookies begged to differ. They made Ali a 7/1 on favourite. Bugner's manager, Andy Smith, reckoned his boy had a 50-50 chance, even if this was only his 29th pro fight. Back in 1970 Smith paid £420 for Bugner to spar with Ali at Clancey's gym in Miami; what with that session and the previous summer's in Dublin, Bugner had spent something like 50 rounds in the ring with Ali. Moreover, gym sources insisted that on those particular occasions Ali couldn't reach Bugner with three blows in succession because of the Briton's upright stance.

Thus, Bugner knew exactly what he was up against. He was getting nine years from Ali and he matched him in height and weight (in fact he proved 1½lb heavier at 15st 9lb). However, could he punch his weight; make it count when he needed to? Said Ali: 'It will be another massacre! Jumbo jets of British are coming to see another St Valentine's Day massacre!' Bugner was unfazed. These theatrics were all too familiar: 'I've heard it all before when I've sparred with him. He has to have a crowd round him and when

(Perry Aghajanoff Collection)

Two thoroughly cheesed-off fighters at the Las Vegas post-fight press conference: Bugner's cut left eye is clearly visible (Mirror Syndication International)

the black Americans come in he naturally turns it on even more. He makes his own rules and breaks all the normal ones. But I treat Ali just like another good turn in the Las Vegas show business programme!' After a 15-minute rant at the weigh-in drew not a single reaction from his impassive opponent Ali conceded verbal defeat: 'I don't seem to be able to get under Bugner's skin. I don't seem to have found the flint to strike.'

Ali did not accomplish the job in hand quite so bloodily as Capone's hitmen had on 14 February 1929 but he did cut Bugner's left eye during the last 20 seconds of the opening round – which probably cost the Englishman dear. As Smith explained to the press: 'We had to change our whole plan when Joe got that bad cut in round one. We had planned for Joe to go after Ali from the start and bang away to his body. Yet in the very first round – zip – his eyebrow was ripped open. When Joe got back to his corner I had to tell him to forget about what we had planned to do and just concentrate on protecting his eye. To do this for 11 rounds against an accurate puncher like Ali was a fine achievement. Joe's not yet 23 and I believe white heavyweights don't come into their prime until they're past 25. Until then, I'm going to nurse him along.' Bugner, for once, finished this instalment of his long-running feud with the British press with more plusses than minuses. In the *Daily Telegraph*, for example, Donald Saunders wrote: 'Bugner pitted his skill and strength against the genius of one of sport's few great artists and has not been found seriously wanting – as most of us thought he would be. Certainly, Bugner was soundly whipped; true, Ali is a fading star. But there are few heavyweights in the world today who would have coped with a difficult problem any better than did the young man about whom so many of us have had so many reservations.'

In point of fact Bugner did come off his stool throwing plenty of leather and was very much the early aggressor. 'He is not fighting in the usual stand-up British style,' reported American commentator Howard Cosell, 'because he learnt his boxing in America, much of it from Muhammad Ali.' By the seventh – Ali's predicted KO round – Bugner's eye was half shut and proceeded to take a fearful battering as a dazzling maelstrom of hooks and uppercuts rained upon it from every conceivable angle. 'Finish this off! Let's go home!' implored Bundini Brown. 'Ring the doorbell, Champ, and go into the house!' Nevertheless, despite shipping all this punishment, Bugner refused to buckle and he greeted the bell with arms triumphantly aloft. And in spite of more of the same in round ten that's how Bugner finished the fight. 'A gallant young man,' was Cosell's verdict. 'We knew he could fight,' added Angelo Dundee. 'He didn't trick us. He tricked a lot of other people but he didn't trick us. The guy made a great fight.'

Bugner's view? 'The eye worried me all the time. I was afraid they might stop it. I didn't realise Ali's legs were as good as they were and he would be so fit. In a way I underestimated him! He was too busy during the fight to talk to me. That seventh round was the round that pleased me most. I proved the stuff he had been spouting about knocking me out in the seventh was just psychological rubbish. And I caught him with a tremendous right cross and I felt myself go right through him.' Ali's response? 'Joe Bugner is a spoiler. If you take him lightly he will step on you. Joe will hit and hurt any other heavyweight but me. He will never meet another dancing like me. Bugner took some of my best punches and he hurt me with a right to the head. I was in a semi-knockout condition. I managed to get out of it because my legs were in such good form. I thought I had him in trouble in the middle rounds but he's got a strong body. Within two years, with added experience, Bugner will be world champion.' As Saunders concluded: 'Hearing those words I wondered whether Ali was preparing the ground for a lucrative return bout.'

Well, February 1975 was to prove not far short of the mark because the return actually took place on 30 June 1975. On this occasion the world title, safely back in Ali's hands since October 1974, was at stake but on this occasion Bugner's effort, in the opinion of most, left much to be desired. As per usual the match was preceded by a drum roll of barely concealed artificiality. Ali was ringside for Bugner's contest with Alberto Lovell in December 1974, providing inter-round 'colour' comment for BBC Radio. He had already entertained the punters once – when he and Britain's new light-heavyweight champion of the world, John Conteh, were introduced in the ring before the main event he yelled: 'You're prettier than me – I gotta bump you off!' Then, at the premature conclusion of what the papers were to describe as 'a travesty of a sporting contest' in round two, Ali leapt on to the ring apron, peeled off his shirt and tie, and issued the time-honoured Ali challenge to 'get-it-on-right-here-and-now!'.

The publicity inevitably linked to an Ali fight coupled with the champion's own inexhaustible need for the attendant flow of 'megabucks' ensured the contest went to one of the attention-seeking developing nations eager to show they could match anything attainable in the West. Datuk Harun, Chief Minister of Malaysia's Selangor state, harboured political ambitions; so, where Djakarta (Indonesia) and Kinshasa (Zaire) led, Kuala Lumpur now followed. However, such a location proved akin to staging the 15 rounds inside one of the hothouses at Kew Gardens. When the two fighters entered the ring, set up in the Merdeka Stadium, the temperature beneath the plastic canopy approached 118 degrees and the humidity was 97 per cent. It was not unreasonable to expect these enervating conditions to wreak greater havoc on the metabolism of a 16st 6lb Caucasian than on a Negro (and a 5lb lighter one) raised in the fetid sub-tropical atmosphere of a Miami gymnasium – an advantage Ali built upon in training by undertaking 15 rounds of non-stop sparring over a 90-minute period using two different partners. Neil Allen, of *The Times*, was suitably awed: 'I

Banging the drum: Ali vacates his commentator's seat at the ringside to goad Bugner, 4 December 1974 (Mirror Syndication International)

MUHAMMAD ALI
vs JOE BUGNER

Kuala Lumpur, Malaysia.
1st. July 75

(Perry Aghajanoff Collection)

believe that the best we can hope for Bugner, and quite possibly the best he subconsciously hopes for himself, is that he will go the full 15 rounds against Ali and end up as a much-admired loser on points. Even if Joe wins he still can't fight.'

Bugner's dehydration problems soon became self-evident: when he tried to take in water between rounds three and four he was physically sick. Nevertheless, his attitude won no points with his auld enemy the British press as the fight ground toward a predictable and overwhelming points decision in Ali's favour: 73/67; 72/65; 74/65. 'Slow-motion Joe just can't cope/Memorably boring/Bugner fought with hardly any conviction/Oh, Joe, why didn't you have a go?' The public also chipped in, peppering the letters column of *Boxing News* with comments along the lines of: 'It made me ashamed to watch our champion/For his 45 minutes of passive resistance Joe received more money than I shall gain in a lifetime/Did the rubber band with which Andy Smith winds him up perish in the heat?' Apart from a brief flurry in the tenth Bugner's sole intention did seem to be survival: hands held high up against his cheekbones, and quick to clinch or grapple at close quarters. In the final round, however, he still found the energy – or was it effrontery – to perform his version of the 'Ali Shuffle'. Confronting his journalistic tormentors head-on, Bugner explained: 'Well, gents, we tried. I'm not going to quit because I've lost to the world heavyweight champion. Without question Muhammad Ali is the greatest athlete in the world. I started out by moving around because I wanted to see what Muhammad's ideas were going to be. After the eighth I thought, "Well, I'll try and step the pace up a bit." Suddenly, I just couldn't find it anywhere. The humidity and the heat just hit me a bit too much.' Questions pertaining to his apparent lack of drive became unrelenting. Bugner's patience finally snapped. 'Get me Jesus Christ, I'll fight him tomorrow!' he blurted out to a room full of journalists, at which Hugh McIlvanney retorted: 'Ah, Joe, you're only saying that because you know He's got bad hands.'

At the age of 25 Bugner was yet to reach his peak. But enough was enough. Contrary to his post-fight statement he did – temporarily at least – quit boxing. The European crown thus fell vacant: the British title, meanwhile, had passed from McAlinden to Bunny Johnson and, on 30 September 1975, to Richard Dunn, regarded as the proud possessor of no more talent and personality than Jack Bodell, the last heavyweight (and another southpaw) hopeful from the stable of George Biddles. Now past his 30th birthday, the Bradford scaffolder and Territorial Army paratrooper had gained a new lease of life upon signing with the veteran Biddles earlier in the year. In 1974 Dunn had lost three times inside four months (two by knockouts) and the end of the road loomed into view. His wife Janet even contacted various boxing journalists and pleaded with them to give her husband a break. Biddles came to the rescue. Once under his wing Dunn immediately rediscovered victory. 'I pride myself in being able to motivate my fighters,' said the canny old manager. 'Hogan Bassey was just a good fighter when he came to me and I made him a world champion. No one gave Jack Bodell a chance against Joe Bugner but we proved them all wrong. I am giving Dunn the same kind of motivation.'

When the referee intervened in the third round of Dunn's fight with Bernd August for the vacant European title on 6 April 1976, the Yorkshireman's seventh straight win ensured entrée to the big league; he was to get a shot at Ali. The venue was Munich's Olympiahalle, setting for the 1972 gymnastics competition. The date: 24 May, three a.m. GMT in order to satisfy American television. Dunn was guaranteed £60,000: 18 months earlier he had been fighting for £300. The war of words was already underway. While Dunn was training for the August fight (in a tent erected on the car park behind Quaglino's Restaurant, in the West End of London), Ali had exploded on to the scene with both matchmaking and mischief in mind. Dunn was disinclined to let Ali steal his long-awaited thunder. Seizing the initiative, he attempted to play on Ali's known fear of flying by telling the champion how many parachute jumps he had made. Quick as a flash Ali jibed: 'Well, then, you should be used to taking a dive!' Dunn's trainer, Jimmy Devanney, was not laughing. 'We've got far too many of these black chat merchants back home in Bradford,' he was freely quoted as saying.

Dunn trained like a madman for the greatest day of his life. Three days before the fight, even, he sparred two rounds, went five rounds on the heavy bag and shadow-boxed for three more! 'I never expected I'd feel so good after such hard training and so close to something as big as this fight,' he informed watching reporters. Dunn tipped the scales at 15st 3lb; Ali weighed in at 15st 10lb, which, significantly, was ten pounds lighter than when he had gained a dull points victory over Jimmy Young just 24 days previously. 'I don't want to look bad again. I let the public down last time.' Lighter or not, the stage on which the weigh-in was being conducted collapsed! Fewer than 7,000 of the 12,000 seats had been sold. The Germans, it was alleged, considered them overpriced (£225 for ringside!) and the Ali camp were reduced to giving tickets away to American servicemen to build a healthy crowd. But, as Neil Allen suggested: 'Ali in the ring against my miniature dachshund Jasper would probably attract a crowd.' No one, of course, gave Dunn a cat-in-hell's chance of lasting the 15 rounds, let alone winning. One nameless wit was heard to say: 'Dunn's got less chance in Munich than Chamberlain had.' Making sport of this likelihood, the *Daily Mirror* arranged for Dunn to undergo a session of hypnosis with the famed television practitioner Romark in an effort to boost his confidence.

Banging the drum: Richard Dunn's turn, 10 March 1976 (Mirror Syndication International)

Dunn was under no illusions. 'I was no fancy dan, just a fighter and it was great to suddenly be on the big merry-go-round, the Ali circus. Ali had tried to wind me up at Quaglino's but I just told him to "F*** off!"; and then he gave me plenty of stick at the press conference in Germany. I enjoyed it! He was a master; it sold tickets. I ignored the press. I'd have committed suicide years ago if I'd taken any notice of them. The only help they gave me was to fire me up, "I'll show the bastards!" kind of thing. I didn't care where the fight was, anywhere in the world would have done, and the time didn't bother me either. I trained just as normal, just a bit more intensively, and didn't have any real game plan. How could you have a game plan against The Greatest? I never professed to be skilful: I just got stuck in. I hoped I could beat him by sheer willpower and determination. I thought he was ready to be taken. He had had some absolute wars. A few fights later Spinks did beat him by sheer guts: I just came a bit too early perhaps. I told myself to go out from the first bell and fight for my life: hit him as much as he hit me. And that's what I did. Toward the end of the second he caught me with a good right and I had to tell myself, "Stay up and hustle him!", but in the third he played right into my hands by starting to dance. I wanted him to dance. While he's doing that he's not throwing punches! I got him in a corner and hurt him so I was very determined at the start of the fourth, but he put me down again. I got up and he put me down again. I kept getting up! You've got to keep fighting. I was all over the place – I thought the fight ended in the fourth until I saw the film! It was bloody hilarious to look at later. At the start of the fifth Ali said to me: "You're going down!", so I replied: "Come on, then!" Going forward was the only way I knew how to fight. Anyway, he had me down again. It's the risk you take when you go in. I made a bit of a cock-up of it but at least I had a go like I promised. I'd not gone all that way for nowt. I'd have kept going: I think the ref stepped in too early. I wanted to go on but the ref is the gaffer. If Ali had been in the same shape for me as he was for Jimmy Young I'm sure I'd have beaten him but he wasn't out of condition for me. Some of the press thought he was and said he wasn't going to treat me seriously, but he did – and that's the main thing. It was a privilege to be in the same ring as The Greatest. He was an unbelievable athlete. If he'd been a ballet dancer he'd still have been the best. I have had dinner with him a couple of times since and have always found him an absolutely brilliant person; a very nice man.'

Referee Herbert Tomser stepped between the two protagonists with 15 seconds of the fifth round to go after Dunn's fifth visit to the canvas. Dunn's pluck, full of traditional Yorkshire grit, won him well-merited plaudits. 'Defiant Dunn – defeated but not discredited' stated *Boxing News*. Even the Yanks were impressed. American television loved the fight (58 million watched it live) because it brought the best out of Ali, and in New York's *Daily News* Dick Young wrote: 'Dunn's determination to try and make a fight of it makes Bugner's showing against Ali look very sad. Sure, Dunn had a glass jaw but he showed guts by the way he kept coming back.' Angelo Dundee went so far as to tell Biddles that Dunn was the toughest of Ali's British opponents; kind, though possibly extravagant, praise, to which The Greatest himself added: 'You got a good fighter there, George. Dunn was no pushover. It was not a mismatch. He shook me twice. It was my new "acupunch" that beat him! He couldn't see it coming. He was better than I thought he'd be. At the end of the third I said to Angie: "I'm glad I took this fight seriously." If I'd been in the same shape as when I fought Jimmy Young I would have lost. I didn't know Dunn hit so hard. I thought he would run but he was better than George Foreman and Joe Bugner, even though he didn't go the distance.' When Dunn and his wife returned to their hotel the 200 or so journalists cramming the lobby burst into spontaneous applause. Wiping a tear from his eye Dunn responded with: 'Give over! Don't be soft!'

One man who continued to believe the contest had been a 'mismatch' was Joe Bugner. 'Someone in his camp should teach Dunn how to protect himself or else he should retire.' The letters page of *Boxing News* was soon inundated with advice for Bugner. 'At least he tried, Joe!' was the bold headline. Stung into action, Bugner promptly abandoned pipe and slippers

Do I get to fight some more of you British if I wear this helmet? (Sport & General)

to settle the issue. Five months later he faced Dunn in the ring. At the sound of the first bell he marched across the ring and planted a right full on Dunn's chin: it was all over in two minutes 14 seconds, the shortest British heavyweight title fight in history. In those 134 seconds Bugner displayed more aggression than he had in 27 rounds with Ali. Then, just as impulsively, he retired yet again. Dunn fought once more (a five-round loss to Kallie Knoetze in South Africa) before calling it a day. There was, however, another, much tougher fight ahead of him. Whilst working on an oil rig he suffered an horrific accident, falling 40 feet and shattering both his legs. Had he not adopted the classic parachutist position on impact, he was told afterwards, he'd have been a dead man. Confined to bed for six months; in a wheelchair for a further nine; then crutches. The experts said he would never walk again.

On 24 October 1978, John L. Gardner assumed the mantle of British champion. Shrewd matchmaker Mickey Duff ('A lot of boxing promoters couldn't match the cheeks of their own backside!') was soon on the scent of a possible meeting with Muhammad Ali, now a palpably ageing and less dangerous opponent – but still sure-fire box office and top-drawer publicity for any young fighter lucky enough to take his scalp. In December 1980 (while Ali was in London to promote the *Freedom Road* movie) Duff announced the fight had been fixed for Tokyo in the New Year. Ali would receive one million pounds and Gardner, who had just earned his biggest purse of £17,500 when knocking out Lorenzo Zanon to retain his European title, was guaranteed £200,000. British boxing was appalled at the prospect. Only two months ago Ali had been hammered to defeat by Larry Holmes. The BBBC quickly voiced its disapproval; in the *News of the World* the much-respected Frank Butler raged: 'This Ali fiasco must be stopped. Surely now, enough is enough.' Japan refused to stage the bout and not even Duff's threat to sue for £300,000 compensation managed to revive the match. Instead, Ali – two months shy of his 39th birthday – climbed through the ropes for what proved to be the final occasion on Friday, 11 December 1981, to fight Commonwealth champion Trevor Berbick in Nassau. The outcome was, sadly, pretty much a foregone conclusion. At the subsequent press conference one American pressman got to his feet and said quietly: 'Muhammad, thank you! You gave us a hell of a ride.'

Fight fans throughout the globe understood and, indeed, shared those simple sentiments. For heavyweight boxers everywhere, and British heavyweights in particular, Gardner's words on being promised the Ali fight were just as apt: 'This fight with Ali is a dream come true for me. Ali did for boxing what the Beatles did for pop music. He made money for boxers all over the world. Now, he's making money for me!'

On 11 December 1981 the gravy train finally ran out of gravy.

PILGRIMAGE

They flocked to Blackwell's from far and wide. Wedged between the White Horse pub and the New Bodleian Library, the cramped Victorian façade of Oxford's premier bookshop suggested too confined a stage for the world's best-known and best-loved sportsman; let alone the world's best-known and best-loved man, period.

His face is as instantly recognised in Soweto as it is in Harlem or Watts. From Tokyo Bay to Whitley Bay they know him; in Times Square and Red Square; on the Copacabana and Bondi; along the boulevards of Paris and among the *bustees* of Calcutta. And of all the places guaranteed to greet this face warmly Britain holds a special spot in its owner's affections. The face they have all come to see on 4 June 1992 belongs to Muhammad Ali aka Cassius Clay, the Louisville Lip, The King, The Champ, The Man. No, let's not pussyfoot around, the face belongs to The Greatest.

Ali was in town, naturally, to promote a book, Thomas Hauser's *Muhammad Ali: His Life and Times*. He was due to arrive at midday. The balding, middle-aged pilgrim who walked into Blackwell's at 11 a.m. found a queue already winding from the sturdy and capacious table laden with copies of the book. He took his place and exchanged pleasantries with those around him: a father dressed more for the beach than a bookshop, accompanied by his small daughter; a garrulous postman, too young to have known The Champ but desperate to meet The Man; a bespectacled student, so slight they'd have to invent a new weight if he were even to contemplate donning boxing gloves. 'How far you come?' enquires the beach-bum in an accent straight from the Mississippi delta.' Oh, about 100 miles, two hours or so driving,' he is informed. 'We're over here on vacation, you know, and couldn't pass up this opp-or-toon-it-ee to meet Muhammad again. I met him in Atlanta after the Quarry fight in '70. Here, I brought some pictures to show him. Just look at these here pictures. My daughter's never met him before, so this is a real special day for her.'

Heads nod graciously at the production of the photographs. They are none too good, but they prove he has met The Man. 'He was The Greatest,' enthuses the student. 'Have you watched the video of the third Frazier fight? That was awesome.' Is he kidding? The Thrilla in Manila: what fight fan above the age of 30 needs to be asked that question? Every minute of the Thrilla in Manila is recorded in the brain for instant replay. Who needs a videotape? Another glance at the watch: it's 11.35, not long to wait now. A smartly dressed female member of staff begs our attention. She is Alyson Hiller, general manager of the books department. 'Ladies and gentlemen, I can assure you Muhammad Ali is on his way. He will meet you all but, and I'm sure you'll understand, his illness makes it impossible for him to quickly sign each and every book as you come to the table, so I have here bookplates signed by him in advance which you may stick into your copy.' The chorus of groans was swelling before she had uttered 'copy'. 'How do we know it's his signature?' piped up the postman. 'Anyone could have written it for him.' A bit near the knuckle to express it so brazenly but, nonetheless, a thought disturbing many another mind in the queue. Still, what the hell? Ali's coming, that's the main thing.

The visit was originally scheduled for the previous September but fell through in mysterious circumstances. Ali had left his home in Berrien Springs, Michigan, on 13 September and was due in England on the 19th; his first important engagement was a £100-a-head charity dinner in aid of the Boxers' Benevolent Fund at the Grosvenor House Hotel, Park Lane, organised by Henry Cooper to mark the 25th anniversary of their 1966 world title fight. When Ali failed to put in an appearance rumours flew thick and fast. It was totally out of character for him not to honour a commitment and disappoint his fans. Was he ill? Had the Parkinson's Syndrome which he had endured for ten years tightened its grip? Fears for his health deepened once it was mentioned he might have run out of medication. Ali was eventually tracked down to the Hotel Intercontinental in Abu Dhabi in the company of former manager Jabir (Herbert) Mohammad and Dr Rashaad Mousoui. 'Muhammad Ali will not come to London,' declared the latter. 'He does not support the book anymore. He is very well and in good health. He has all his medicine. Everything he needs.' Robson Books Ltd, the book's publisher, professed astonishment. Ali had co-operated with Hauser over a period of two years during the researching and writing of the book and had already participated in a two-week promotional tour in the USA. However, it was suggested elsewhere that certain of Ali's associates were less than pleased at some of the book's references to them and had pressurised him into withholding further endorsement.

The Man finally arrives at Blackwell's Bookshop, Oxford, 4 June 1992 (Oxford Mail)

Whatever actually lay behind Ali's non-appearance in 1991 he had at least made it to England this time. He arrived on 26 May – direct from the USA, which facilitated matters – accompanied by his wife Lonnie and twin daughters Rasheeda and Jamillah, and had checked in at the Cumberland Hotel, near Marble Arch. Almost his first port of call was Homerton Hospital in the East End where British super-middleweight Michael Watson was recovering in the neurological rehabilitation ward from injuries sustained during his world title fight with Chris Eubank ten

months earlier. Watson had undergone three operations to remove blood clots from his brain and repair damaged vessels; for a month after the fight he had been comatose and on a ventilator. Progress was slow but at last he could conduct a simple conversation. Ali had kept in close touch with the case and hoped his visit would assist the British boxer's recovery process. As he entered Watson's room the stricken fighter clenched a fist in salute. Ali returned the salute as only he could: 'You are almost as pretty as I am.'

The debt of honour to Henry Cooper was also quickly repaid. The two former adversaries met at a charity dinner on 2 June and posed for the obvious photograph – 'Enery's 'Ammer in contact with Ali's chin. But they've long since become friends and Ali attended the 50th birthday celebrations of the Cooper twins in May 1984. 'Ali was the greatest personality of the boxing world for the last 50 years,' insists Cooper. 'No heavyweight could move like Ali, nor ever will, because they are like battleships nowadays. He had cat-like reflexes.'

Ali's noon deadline comes and goes with still no sign of him. The queue now snakes round the book-cased walls, past cookery and hardback fiction, and has tumbled out on to the pavements of Broad Street. If Alyson Hiller and marketing executive Jenny Urwin are growing anxious no one guesses. Yet the two of them have good cause. The very first signing they had organised was the non-event of last September! 'We had kept in touch with Robson's and spoken only the previous day, so we knew he was coming,' confides Jenny. 'Though we were only going to believe it when we saw him. Our major worry on the day was the queuing and trying to keep everybody happy. The layout of the shop means it only takes one or two browsers in some aisles to cause a blockage.'

Suddenly bedlam breaks loose. A white Rover 827 has drawn up outside. Traffic grinds to a halt; tourists forget the Sheldonian Theatre opposite and cross the road for a better view. Inside the shop a hundred necks crane for that first, confirmatory glimpse of The Man. The spotlights surrounding the table intended for Ali are switched on and an unsightly scrum promptly develops as a posse of photographers, TV cameramen and radio reporters fight for a prime position. The seasoned pros among their number unfold stools and clamber on to them. Just like the old days: just like it always was. Pandemonium. Ali has arrived and his very presence was always guaranteed to induce mayhem. The tall, bearded figure of Howard Bingham, Ali's long-time confidant and personal photographer, comes into view followed by the curly-haired Thomas Hauser and Ali's aide Mustafa. Then Ali. Moving tentatively, slightly hunched, eyes freeze-focused as if on some distant horizon or memory; no smile illuminates that famous mahogany face – yet. In contrast to Bingham and Hauser who are dressed casually Ali is attired like the ambassador he has become:

You will all get your chance, be patient (Jeannette Tanner)

statesmanlike blue suit, crisp white shirt, colourful silk tie. Slowly and deliberately he removes his jacket and settles into his chair.

The first man in the queue is Alan Smith. He was standing by the table at 9.30 a.m. determined to be first. Smith runs a pizza delivery service in Oxford. He is 55 and has suffered with Parkinson's disease for nine years. He gets up nervously from the chair Alyson Hiller had thoughtfully provided him with and is guided towards Ali who rises to greet him. The emotion floods into Smith's eyes as Ali shakes his hand. They hold a copy of the book between them for the sake of the cameras. Ali whispers something in Smith's ear and it looks as if he might break down and cry. The heart bleeds. This day must mean more to him than anyone else here. 'I have always admired him as a boxer, but since his illness I suppose I identify with him much more. We chatted about some of the treatments he was taking.'

As the initial explosion of flashbulbs, curiosity and media pleas of 'This way, Ali! Please, Ali! This way!' subsides, Ali attacks the job in hand and the line begins to move. Quite soon he comes eyeball to eyeball with his old acquaintance from Atlanta. 'Look at these pictures, Muhammad. Do you recognise it? It's you and me after the Quarry fight. I gotta poster here of you, Muhammad. Can you sign it for me?' Mustafa accepts the poster and unrolls it on to the table. Ali signs, as slowly and deliberately as he had removed his jacket. 'We can check the signature now,' says the queue's resident Doubting Thomas. 'Gee, that's great, Muhammad. This is my daughter Toni.' Ali's face lightens as he catches sight of the first child of the day and he pats her neatly brushed hair with a father's gentle touch.

It's the postman's turn next. For what seems the first time this day he is lost for words. The lips are moving yet nothing discernible issues forth. Ali frequently has this effect on people. The middle-aged man was determined he would not be struck dumb when the moment he had craved for as long as he could remember finally came about. Something pertinent would have to be said, however unoriginal, to make the most of the occasion. He steps forward and reaches for the hand extended toward him. It is not as large a fist as he'd imagined, not the vice it once was of course, and its skin is as soft and smooth as that of the face meeting his gaze: the best-known face in the world. 'Champ, I've waited 30 years to meet you, ever since the first Cooper fight.' The seeds of a grin start to crease Ali's features. He is not one to forego the opportunity of responding to this variation of an old and trusted line. 'Thirty years, eh? You must be really old,' he whispers as the Radio Oxford reporter pushes her microphone between the two men in a frantic attempt to capture the exchange. 'That's for sure, Champ,' replies the pilgrim, 'but unlike you I ain't pretty anymore.' Ali's grin widens into a full-blown smile, revealing a wonderfully bright and neat set of front teeth but, in truth, the real smile beams from eyes which have sparkled into animation. The facial muscles may not flex like they used to but those nut-brown eyes still run the gamut of emotions. A word from Alyson Hiller brings the magic interlude to a close. It's the turn of someone else's dream to come true.

By the end of a one and a half hour session Ali had shaken over 300 hands and kissed dozens of toddlers. 'I am not really a boxing fan,' said Monica Mutz, whose two-year-old Kerry was a particular favourite. 'I think it is his humanity I most admire.' Nor was Andy Saxton, Oxford's Commonwealth Games weightlifting gold medalist, a boxing fanatic: 'But I had to meet him. He was such a fantastic sportsman.' And the book? Blackwell's sell 612 copies. What with over 100 reserve orders for those unable to attend it amounts to £13,000 worth. 'Far better than most,' declares Jenny Urwin. 'For a political memoir, like Norman Tebbit's for instance, we'd only sell 200 or so. It was all a bit of a blur but for us it was a really good signing.'

Afterwards Ali and his entourage are ushered upstairs to the boardroom where a traditional *après*-signing repast comprising the best canapes and delicately cut sandwiches Marks & Spencer can offer has been laid out. Ali takes one look at the feast and gestures to Mustafa: 'Muhammad wonders whether he could have a burger and some fries.' Though unaware of the

First man in the queue – Alan Smith has been waiting three hours (Jeannette Tanner)

reason for the hasty order, McDonald's are pleased to oblige.

During this informal lunch some of Blackwell's staff have the opportunity to meet Ali. To two of the shop's greatest Ali fans, Rodney Smith and James Blackburn, had fallen the task of unpacking all the books. They are introduced; Ali sits them down and shares his burger and fries. In mock anger at Rodney's appetite Ali curls his lip and delivers a playful punch to the solar plexus. Smith and Blackburn feel a strange mixture of pride and pain. Pride at this privileged moment of intimacy with an idol; pain at his cruelly reduced circumstances. 'For someone whose way with words was always as notable as his way with his fists the fact that the simplest of utterances now requires an agonising effort must be the ultimate frustration,' observed James. 'So he sat, absorbed in his own thoughts, as conversation flowed all around him.' When saying thank you for the lunch and all the good times past Blackburn is rewarded with one of Ali's current *bon mots*, one heavy on irony and not a little sorrow: 'Man, I'm going back in the ring.'

Lunch over, Ali is given a tour of the shop and he is especially impressed by the extensive religious section in the vast subterranean Norrington Room. He is presented with two volumes which take his eye. Alyson Hiller also receives an unexpected bonus. When duty calls her back to the shop floor her departure is marked by a kiss on the cheek from Ali. 'I was in a daze afterwards: it was all too overwhelming. When I was younger he was winning all his titles and everyone knew him and he was a hero to us all. We have had Booker Prize-winners and all sorts to do signings and you can become blasé about them; but I made it very clear to everyone that I would be around for this one! And the way he behaved with Rodney and Jim really lived up to his hero status. It was a totally private meeting with no publicity angle whatsoever. It's just amazing how someone that big – and, it must be said, ill – could take so much trouble.'

Understandably, Ali eventually showed signs of wilting. It's a hot day, he is no longer invulnerable and, after all, the tour is in its tenth day and fifth city. Manchester, Leeds, Nottingham, London, Oxford; Birmingham, Croydon and London (again) still to be visited. 'His condition has been constant for four years but he has good and bad days depending on the jet-lag,' Hauser explained. 'His condition is not degenerative, though, because he's not getting hurt anymore. But he just loves being Muhammad Ali, he loves the response he gets and draws strength from these people here today.' Indeed, when the last satisfied customer wandered away clutching their literary memento Ali's eyes continued to prowl in search of another. This was his stage. Perhaps, instead of a money-making torture chamber Blackwell's had been a pleasuredome. Those occasional smiles – flashing and incomparable as of old – seemed to say as much.

'Yes, it is a bit sad seeing him like this,' philosophised the student, 'but I

'Champ, I've waited 30 years to meet you . . .'
'Thirty years, eh? You must be really old.' (Jeannette Tanner)

think a lot of people misunderstand his illness. His mind is clear. We shouldn't underestimate him. What you are seeing is a lot of people remembering the good times. Who else would we stand here and do this for?'

He volunteered Gorbachev as about the only other person. The pilgrim disagreed. Only The Greatest could have lured him here.